WHAT A SH!T SHOW!

BEYOND ILLNESS AND THE COURAGE
IT TOOK TO REDESIGN MY LIFE

NICOLE TRIMBOLI

First published by Ultimate World Publishing 2025
Copyright © 2025 Nicole Trimboli

ISBN

Paperback: 978-1-923425-87-3
Ebook: 978-1-923425-88-0

Nicole Trimboli has asserted her rights under the Copyright, Designs and Patents Act 1988 to be identified as the author of this work. The information in this book is based on the author's experiences and opinions. The publisher specifically disclaims responsibility for any adverse consequences which may result from use of the information contained herein. Permission to use information has been sought by the author. Any breaches will be rectified in further editions of the book.

All rights reserved. No part of this publication may be reproduced, stored in or introduced into a retrieval system, or transmitted in any form, or by any means (electronic, mechanical, photocopying, recording or otherwise) without the prior written permission of the author. Any person who does any unauthorised act in relation to this publication may be liable to criminal prosecution and civil claims for damages. Enquiries should be made through the publisher.

Cover design: Ultimate World Publishing
Layout and typesetting: Ultimate World Publishing
Editor: Victoria Pickens

Ultimate World Publishing
Diamond Creek,
Victoria Australia 3089
www.writeabook.com.au

Foreword

Watching one of your best friends face a life-altering diagnosis and come to terms with it, has been incredibly moving. Nicole has had to make immense sacrifices; not only to overcome cancer, but to give herself the best chance at recovery, even when choices were unimaginably difficult.

Seeing Nicole refuse to let this define her, make incredibly tough decisions, and emerge on the other side shinning brighter than ever, has been truly inspiring. She could have easily let this break her, but her resilience and courage, and above all her unwavering positivity and radiant smile, have been a testament to her incredible strength. I am so unbelievably proud of her.

Emma Smith

Seeing you now, compared to where you were when your journey started, is nothing but remarkable. Juggling the responsibilities of a demanding corporate career, being a single parent, and having to manage two children along with the multiple roles that come with that is truly inspiring. But with all of that came the challenge of what you've been through, and how you needed to walk away from almost everything in your life to make sure you were here today to tell the story. In itself, that is strength.

Nicole Atherton

Disclaimer

This autobiography is a personal account of my life, thoughts, and experiences. The content herein is based on my own memories and interpretations and may not reflect events with complete factual accuracy. While I have made every effort to be truthful, memory is inherently subjective, and some details may have been altered, omitted, or reconstructed for narrative clarity or privacy.

Names, locations, and identifying details of certain individuals have been changed or anonymised to protect their privacy. Any similarity to actual persons, living or deceased, or actual events is purely coincidental, unless explicitly stated.

This work is not intended to defame, harm, or misrepresent any individual, group, organisation, or entity. The views expressed are solely my own and do not represent the views of any other person, institution, or organisation.

To the fullest extent permitted by law in Australia, I disclaim all liability for any loss, damage, or distress caused to any person or entity as a result of the content of this book. This publication is provided for personal reflection and general interest and is not intended to provide legal, medical, or professional advice.

Contents

Foreword	3
Disclaimer	5
Introduction	9
Dedication	11
1. When Everything Changed	15
2. Stillness in the Storm	23
3. Love, Loss, and Who Stayed	33
4. The Words No One Wants to Hear	41
5. Held Together by Kindness	53
6. Bag Blow Outs, Poonami's, and Laughing Anyway!	61
7. When Goodbye Becomes a Kindness	73
8. Tired but Trying	83
9. The Gift Alone Without Being Lonely	93
10. Loving Myself Outloud	101
11. Becoming Someone New	109
12. Feedback, What Others See and What I Know	117
13. Everything I Was, Everything I Now Am	127
Afterword	135
About the Author	139
Nicole Trimboli	143
Speaker Bio	143
References	147
Acknowledgements	149

Introduction

This book began with a life that slowly became overwhelming as I tried to be everything to everyone, neglecting the one person I should have cared for most—myself. It wasn't until serious illness stopped me in my tracks. It was only then I truly understood the real toll of neglecting my physical, mental and emotional well-being. Now, having found peace and balance, I've realised that coming out the other side of illness isn't just about physical recovery; it's about the deep healing of mind, body and soul.

It will be revealed that real, lasting wellness goes far beyond simply treating the body. It requires a shift in how we view ourselves, our mental health, and the way we approach life itself. In this book, I'm sharing the lessons and tools I've discovered as I worked through the physical, mental and emotional challenges that accompanied my struggles. These aren't lessons I learnt easily, but they are the keys to reclaiming your well-being one small change at a time.

For much of my life, I believed that pushing harder, going faster, and ignoring the signs of burnout was the way to succeed. I lived with a sense that bad things happened to other people, not me. That was until illness forced me to confront the way I was living. It is a lesson I wish I'd understood sooner: health, *true* health, cannot be bought, and it's far more valuable than anything money can ever provide.

My journey has been a massive wake-up call, one I didn't listen to the first time, and while I can't change the past, I can offer you something different. You now have the chance to recognise the importance of mental and emotional health before life demands that you do. By reading this book, you are already taking the first step toward a healthier, more balanced version of yourself.

In my professional life, I've achieved success and I have achieved personal goals, but I have come to realise that nothing is more precious than good health. We often overlook this until it's threatened, and it's only then that we truly understand its value. This book is about shifting that perspective.

Writing this has been a deeply emotional experience for me revisiting some of the hardest times in my life while also celebrating how far I've come. It's a reminder that healing is not just one thing, but it's always possible. I'm grateful to be able to share my journey with you, and I hope it inspires you to embrace your own path to a well future mind, body, and soul.

I don't like to use the term "coach" because I believe it implies someone who shouts from the sidelines. I'm here as someone who walks beside you, offering guidance with kindness and patience as you make the changes necessary for better mental and physical well-being. This is a journey that requires time, compassion, and understanding. It's about progress, not perfection, and we're in it together.

Dedication

To my beautiful children, you've shown me strength beyond your years, enduring so much with kindness and resilience. No parent wants their child to witness their illness, but I hope you've learnt from my journey. Life changes constantly, and embracing change is key to happiness. Take care of your mind, body, and soul as health cannot be bought. Travel, learn, and experience life to the fullest. I love you both very much. Watching you grow and start to create the life of your dreams fills me with so much pride. This is for you.

To my parents, whose unwavering support is endless, words can never fully express my gratitude. Mum, thank you for stepping in and giving so much of yourself, and Dad, for always being my objective sounding board no matter the subject. Thank you for driving me to each gruelling chemo session without hesitation, even when it was hardest for you. You both have been my shining lights in my darkest moments. This is for you.

To my sister, who dropped everything to be there for me. Your love, help and dedication to me and my children is never ending. Moving into my home, providing meals, parenting in my absence, driving teenagers around during a time of chaos means more to me than you'll ever know. Through all of this our love and respect for each other has reached new heights, my heart is forever grateful. This is for you.

To my soul sisters, I am privileged to call you my friends, your love, support, and belief in me has been invaluable. Each of you in your own way have held space for me and given selflessly to provide all the things I needed. Endless phone calls, lots of hugs and tears and laughter shared, a complete relocation, spiritual support, you have listened and guided me through some of the most difficult times. Always lifting me up into what is truly now the best place ever. This is for you.

To all my friends, past work colleagues, clients and extended family that have followed and supported my journey, and that amazing friend who sent me to the doctors that day and saved me. Some of you have supported me spiritually and some with kindness, help and faith along the way. This is for you.

To the people who have passed through my life up until now. Although not everyone has stayed with me. Each of these individuals are deeply valued for what they have contributed to my life. These are past friends and partners, I am grateful and thank you all for walking alongside me during the hard battles. Your love and support carried me through some of the darkest days I have ever faced. This is for you.

To my love our future is so bright. My heart is full, and I am beyond grateful for the endless love and support you provide me with, the grounding and continuous belief in me that you give unconditionally. You truly are the adventure I didn't know I needed to have. This is for you.

This book is a heartfelt gift to each of you, a tribute to what you've shared with me. My gratitude is endless.

Nurturing your mind, body, and soul brings balance,
because good health is priceless
— **Nicole Trimboli**

1

When Everything Changed

This was the moment everything shifted — from niggling symptoms to a life-altering diagnosis. This chapter sets the stage for a journey of fear, clarity, and unexpected strength.

I was the last person to ever believe that I would meditate, and I'm ashamed to say that before my diagnosis I didn't truly believe in having mental health problems.

I believed that I should push myself until I couldn't push myself anymore because that's how I achieve goals. I believed in not taking time out for myself. The harder I worked, the more money I would make, the better my life would be, and that being tired was a sign of weakness, success was progression above all.

I never thought that looking after your mental health was real. I honestly thought that people used it as an excuse—even after watching a close family member struggle with this when I was a teen. Well that was until it happened to me. I never knew anything about burnout. I'd never even heard of burnout. Back in the 90s it was referred to as executive stress, and you never wanted to admit to anyone you had that as there was such a stigma attached to it.

I was working almost full time again whilst pregnant with my second child and I was so determined to show everyone how amazing I was and was secretly planning to get back to work within four weeks of his birth. I know now this should never have been my focus; it should have been to bond with my beautiful newborn and spend time with my two children at home enjoying our family. This was not possible due to financial pressures and commitments at home. It was so important to keep money coming into our household. Taking too much time off work meant that we may need to downsize our home in order to reduce the financial burden. This was not an option… well not in my mind anyway.

I was living in a world of judgement, and my internal dialogue was working overtime asking me what would everyone think? Telling me I had to make sure I was appearing to be career successful, keep a clean and tidy showroom standard family home. And now I was completing the picture by adding the perfect little family to that home. Putting more pressure on myself and listening to my internal dialogue I was pushing the envelope more than ever.

I now had a two-month-old baby, and I would be breastfeeding standing up while I was stirring something on the stove for dinner, cutting up vegetables on the bench while my two-year-old was running around. I also had the bath running, trying to coordinate bath time and get a meal on the table so that everyone was in bed at a reasonable time, this was just a typical day in my life as a mum.

Once the children were in bed, I was folding, washing, putting another load of laundry on, making lunches for the family ready for the next day, all while trying to process what I had just experienced during my workday, which was often very stressful. It didn't help that I was so hard on myself and would dwell on things that people said to me or tasks that I felt might have required more attention. These things would weigh on me well into the night, into my dreams and would wake me up. I would be thinking of solutions to problems at work and reducing costs for the company.

I realised one night I was sleeping with such tensed muscles throughout my body, my teeth were clenched, and I was waking with my hands squeezed into fists. Headaches and migraines were constant with my neck muscles always in knots.

It was probably at this stage while I was standing at the stove stirring the dinner, just contemplating all of the crazy, I started to ask myself is this it? Is this is what my life has become? I come home make dinner, bath the kids get them off to bed maybe read them a story. Trying so hard to have all of this happen in a reasonable time frame to ensure they were not too tired the next morning. Then once everyone was settled and happy the house was quiet, my real work would begin, cleaning up in the kitchen, tidying up of the house, emptying the bath, putting everyone's clothes in the wash. These are just things that we do as mums that we don't even think about. But it is a big, big job on top of a job that I was doing five days a week, nine to five, and sometimes I didn't always walk out of my nine to five on time. Most days the leftover stress, questions and baggage from the day would follow me home, along with my laptop, as I was often communicating with other colleagues and customers in international time zones, responding to emails and phone calls out of hours.

I would usually sit down at around nine o'clock at night, and I don't think my food even had time to digest in my stomach, I was shovelling food in so that I could hurry up and get everything done and cleaned up so I could go to bed. I would just collapse into bed, unable to switch my brain off, trying to get to sleep, knowing, oh my gosh, I've only got so many hours before I have to get up and it all starts again. I would open my eyes in the morning and think to myself, "Okay, deep breath. Nicole. Here we go. Here we go." Here goes another day I was living Groundhog Day. It was just one day melting into the next, the weekends were filled with social engagements, where the children had to look perfectly dressed. When I took them out, I put all this pressure on myself to make sure everyone looked perfect and that we were displaying the perfect little family, ensuring that the kids were behaving all the while trying to spend time with them. I never really got to spend a lot of time with them. The flow on from that was I would beat myself up and feel guilty about that too. So not only was I carrying the week's workday with me on the weekend, I was carrying mum guilt, which every working mother has, and, not having time to sit and do things with my children because I was too busy doing household chores and running around, trying to be everything to everybody and organise things.

I was shell of a person, and I was just existing. I didn't know who I was. The only thing that was driving me was more money and success at work, and everything else in my life seemed like such a burden and such a hassle, and all I knew was exhaustion and I had no joy. There was no fun. I lost the ability to laugh. I didn't even notice what I was becoming. I was angry and negative all the time. I forgot how to make fun of myself, or even look at myself as being a fun person. The only time I was fun was when I had a few drinks, and that was because I never allowed myself to relax, so after a few wines then I became a fun person to be around, which looking back now, was very toxic behaviour.

I lost purpose, direction and had no real goals or personal aspirations in my life. I didn't realise it at the time, but I was just about to hit rock bottom round one.

At this point in my life my health and general wellbeing was always bad. I was struggling all round due to lifestyle and lack of self care. I was overweight because I was eating unhealthy food and drinking copious amounts of alcohol to cope with my busy life. I was self-medicating and didn't even know how to relax. I knew one speed, and that was fast, straight ahead, and no sleep. And I kept going and going because I had to appear to look like super woman, super mum. I felt It was an expectation of the world around me to just keep pushing through because that's what great women did and I wanted to be not just any woman but an amazing woman. So I continued to do this because in my world that's what women did.

We all worked full time, ran a tight household, had a beautiful home that was kept clean and tidy. We all had the perfect little family, all while running kids around to play dates, childcare and all sorts of things, and just trying to be present like we were the perfect parents.

Inside I was screaming!

I didn't even realise, but I was constantly searching for a better, easier way. I was trying to claw my way out, it felt impossible I was the main income earner in the family, and my husband, at the time, would help during the week and on the weekends with the kids. He was tired too and his way of relaxing was spending time on the couch, TV or music—he had a way of being able to take himself away and escape with these things he enjoyed. I had this ideal in my head that if I just kept pushing and pushing, everthing would be perfectly clean and tidy. It was just this cycle and like a massive hamster wheel that I just could not get off.

I was trapped!

Then the universe, stepped in and it pushed me off the edge of life as I knew it.

It happened while we were holidaying with friends in Adelaide over Christmas. At the time, my eldest child was two, and youngest child was five months old. It was hot, I was extremely overweight, leading up to the holiday season and our trip to Adelaide, I'd had a few niggling aches and pains. I had some neck and back pain, which I chose to ignore in favour of attending a Christmas party for work one evening. I ended up so uncomfortable and in pain that we left and headed home early. I was also experiencing extreme sweating at night. At the time I was getting really hot and waking up wet, covered in sweat, but still I pushed through. Visiting the doctors a few times, complaining that I was tired and feeling unwell and that I had neck, back and shoulder pain, the doctor recommended I go and see a physio or have a massage as he put it down to having a toddler, a baby and lack of sleep. So I went and did this before we went on holidays, with no great relief.

I pushed on and we went on holidays. I remember it clearly standing there, something I'll never forget, in the caravan park with the kids playing out the front of our cabin, I put my hand on my neck and felt an egg sized lump in the ditch between my neck and my collarbone on my left-hand side.

Everyone I was holidaying with at the time tried to make light of it and make me feel better by dismissing it and saying 'it could be a gland', or it could 'just be some swelling or something'. I think instinctively I knew something was wrong because of the symptoms I had leading up to finding the lump.

We continued on with our trip, and when I got back, I spoke to a few people about it and tried to make a doctor's appointment, however being public holidays I couldn't get in for quite a few days, so I had to wait it out.

I finally went to my doctor's appointment, and I remember sitting in the doctor's office when he said to me, "Well, Nicole, it's one of two things." He said, "It's either an infected gland, which I really don't think it is, or it's cancer." He just said it and laid it on me right then and there. Then he sent me off to undergo a myriad of blood tests and very invasive biopsy of the lump. I had previously had blood tests which had shown all clear results. Nothing showed up previously when I went to the doctors telling him that I was tired and have a sore neck and back. The next step was to have a CT scan and MRI, and so it began. This all took weeks which felt like months to get appointments then some more waiting and anxiety until finally the results came back, and I was positively diagnosed with Hodgkin's Lymphoma. It was cancer!

The moment of realisation happened for me when I got into the car by myself, I burst into tears all alone. I knew I was sick, really sick the panic had set in right at that moment, would I live or die? I had small children. I couldn't bare the thought of what might be, my two childrens innocent little faces flashed before my eyes, it was unbearable and the tears flowed down my cheeks. I slowly pulled myself together. I then vowed to myself that from that minute on, I was going to fight, and not just any fight I was going to fight with everything I had in me, really hard in order to stay there for my children. Because I was not going to leave them without a mother, I was absolutely terrified.

2

Stillness in the Storm

In the chaos of appointments and anxiety, meditation became more than a practice, it became a lifeline. The lesson of finding inner silence and the effect it can have on the most overactive minds.

When I first encountered meditation, I had no idea what it was. In fact, my first true meditation experience happened in the middle of my life-threatening battle—during my first round of chemotherapy for Hodgkin's lymphoma. I was so overwhelmed by the physical and mental toll of my treatment that I would often find myself violently sick with worry, nausea, and fear before each session. My body was locked in stress, and my mind was consumed with the trauma of what was happening to me. I couldn't stop the cycle of vomiting. It was the psychological weight of the situation, more than the physical, that caused the sickness. My mental health was failing fast. There was nothing medical offered to assist me or any other patients with this trauma response. The only thing offered was additional drugs to dull the senses, to not feel the mental effect. This was a here and now solution to stop the vomiting but not a long-term solution for healing the trauma of my treatment.

To assist in controlling the trauma vomiting I was taken in for each treatment and quickly canulated (put on a drip) so the nurses could administer Phenergan a drug that gave me a horrible taste in my mouth and eventually hit me hard enough to make me sleep. This was all before they administered the real drugs bag after bag of the poisonous chemotherapy drugs. Due to the fact I was extremely tense and stressed upon arrival I remember vividly the Phenergan hit my body with a jolt and then the jitters and restlessness began. The Phenergan made me sleepy but still lucid enough to be able to get up and go to the toilet as I needed to be able to pass the litres and litres of chemotherapy drugs going through me with toilet visits about every 40 minutes. Recounting this even now gives me nausea just reliving the details.

It was in this state of chaos that I unknowingly discovered the transformative power of meditation. I had no idea at the time, but through sheer desperation, I started to create a mental escape. I would lay in the hospital bed, and begin prior to the Phenergan being administered and then receiving my treatments. I began to mentally transport myself to a place where I felt safe, calm, and peaceful – a beach. I imagined the sand under my feet, the sound of the waves crashing, the warmth of the sun on my skin, and the distant call of seagulls. This mental imagery gave me control when I had none over the harsh reality of the treatment. Over time, I became able to escape into that space, and I noticed each time I did this prior to receiving the Phenergan it was reducing the bolt of the drug hitting me hard. It was putting me in a state whereby I was receiving the drug calmly and the effect was reducing the jittering and restlessness down each time. The deeper I could get my breathing and take my mind elsewhere, the easier and calmer it made the brutal process of receiving all of the drugs during chemotherapy… it became more bearable.

This wasn't just a distraction, it was a form of meditation. But at the time, I didn't realise that was what it was. Meditation was not as mainstream back then, and I was just doing what I could to cope. Looking back, I now realise that this simple act of calming my mind was a profound practice that helped me survive each of those dark days in that old hospital ward whilst receiving lifesaving chemotherapy.

Meditation, as I now understand it, is a practice that involves calming the mind, focusing attention, and cultivating awareness. It is a tool that can bring clarity, calmness, and emotional balance. Meditation isn't limited to sitting in a quiet room with your eyes closed; it can take many forms. For me, it started with mental imagery, allowing my mind to drift away from the trauma of chemotherapy. The act of focusing on the beach, the waves, and my breath served as an anchor.

Many people think meditation is about erasing all thoughts, but that's not the case. It's about noticing your thoughts and learning to let them flow without judgment. Whether you're focusing on your breath, a mantra, or simply observing the world around you, the practice allows you to break free from mental chatter and create space for stillness.

The benefits of meditation are now widely recognised, and research has shown its powerful impact on mental, emotional, and even physical health.

A meta-analysis published in *Psychological Science* has shown that meditation can improve emotional regulation, enhance concentration, and reduce stress. In Australia, interest in meditation continues to rise. According to the Australian Bureau of Statistics' National Health Survey (2017–18), approximately 2.1 million Australians—around 10% of the population—reported practising meditation in the past year. More recent data from a 2023 national representative survey also highlights a growing uptake, with researchers noting "a continued increase in the use of meditation and mindfulness practices across all age groups". These findings reflect a broader cultural shift towards preventative mental health strategies and holistic wellbeing.

For me, meditation became an essential tool to deal with the physical and emotional challenges of illness. It wasn't just about surviving chemotherapy; it was about maintaining a sense of inner peace and emotional balance during an incredibly difficult time. And while the side effects of my treatment were still very real, meditation helped me cope with the emotional toll that was far harder to manage.

Looking back at my experience, I can't help but wonder: what if I had never discovered meditation? What if I hadn't taken that mental journey to the beach each time I entered the hospital? Would I have been able to cope with the overwhelming nature of chemotherapy and its side effects? What if meditation hadn't helped me regulate my mind and body during such an intense time?

What if we all took time out each day to check in with our mental and emotional health, to give ourselves the space to breathe, to pause, and to clear our minds?

This is where meditation can be a game-changer in everyday life. In a world where we are constantly on the go, overwhelmed by stress, and inundated with responsibilities, taking time to reset is crucial. We all face moments of anxiety, stress, and overwhelm. Meditation isn't a cure-all, but it is an incredibly effective tool for managing these emotions and fostering resilience.

I've found that when life becomes too busy, when I feel overwhelmed by my schedule or the weight of other people's expectations, I start to lose that grounding I've worked so hard to maintain. These moments are a signal that it's time for me to step back, take a deep breath, and practice what I know works: slowing down, reconnecting with myself, and re-centring.

Life, especially when busy, can be like trauma to the body, constant pressure that can lead to exhaustion and burnout. In those moments, I now to recognise the signs of mental overload and make time for joy, for calm, for rest. Whether it's a walk on the beach, a few minutes looking out the window, or just breathing deeply, I give myself the space to reset. It's a daily practice, and like any muscle, the more we practice, the easier it becomes to tap into that sense of calm, even in the chaos.

Years later, after my second round of chemotherapy, I realised the importance of meditation in my healing journey. This time, I took it a step further. I enrolled in meditation and holistic counselling training, eager to learn more about the practice that had so profoundly impacted my life. By becoming a qualified meditation teacher and holistic counsellor, this now allows me to not only deepen my personal practice but to help others discover the same peace and balance.

Through this work, I see the transformative power of this simple practice. It has helped people cope with illness, anxiety, stress, and even trauma, much like it helped me all those years ago and is still helping me today in daily life.

It was during my study that I discovered, my instinctive coping strategy had real scientific backing.

Meditation is a journey, not a destination. It's a practice that requires consistency, patience, and self-compassion. And it's not just something we do when life gets hard – it's a tool for enhancing our overall wellbeing and living a life of greater peace and balance.

According to the 2020 Australian Community Survey, over half of Australians (57%) express preference for the spiritual practice of spending time in nature and the outdoors. Just under half (47%) prefer listening to music that moves them or lifts their spirits; and around a third (32%) nominate prayer, meditation and mindfulness practices as a preferred choice.

As I continue moving forward with a much healthier lifestyle, I remind myself that life will always bring its challenges but I now have the tools to navigate those challenges with more ease. I am not perfect, and I still struggle at times with the pull of a busy schedule or the stress of external pressures. I have learnt the importance of not being so reactive to people and situations, taking time to breathe, to check in with myself, and to step back when needed. It's a constant practice, but one that has given me the resilience to face anything that comes my way.

Integrating meditation into daily life can lead to significant improvements in mental and physical health. My personal experience underscores its transformative power. I encourage others to explore meditation, whether through guided sessions or personal practices, to discover its benefits firsthand.

So, if you're reading this, I encourage you to find your own version of peace, whether through meditation, mindfulness, or simply taking a moment each day to pause. It's one of the most important gifts you can give yourself.

This chapter is not just a reflection of my own experience but an invitation for you to explore the benefits of meditation in your own life. *"If meditation helped me find peace in my darkest moments, imagine what it could do for you. Why not try it today?"*

Dr. Herbert Benson: Meditation Research Pioneer

In the late 1960s, Dr. Herbert Benson of Harvard Medical School conducted scientific studies to test the health benefits of meditation. He determined that meditation could be used successfully in treating physiological problems, such as high blood pressure, heart disease, and migraine headaches, as well as autoimmune diseases, such as diabetes and arthritis. As they meditated, he found that his test subjects' heartbeats and breathing had slowed, their blood lactate levels decreased, and their brains had increased in alpha activity, which is a sign of relaxation. Dr. Benson also found that meditation was helpful in stopping or slowing obsessive thinking anxiety, depression, and hostility. His extensive research on the effects of meditation, leading to the identification of the "relaxation response." This response is characterised by a series of physiological changes that counteract the body's stress-induced fight-or-flight reaction. In his studies, Dr. Benson observed that individuals practising meditation experienced:

- ***Decreased metabolism***

- ***Slower heart rate***

- ***Reduced blood pressure***

- ***Slower breathing rate***

- ***Increased alpha brain-wave activity,*** *indicative of a state of relaxation*

These findings suggest that meditation can play a significant role in reducing stress and promoting overall well-being. Moreover, Dr. Benson's research indicates that meditation can help alleviate conditions exacerbated by stress, such as high blood pressure, insomnia, and anxiety.

In essence, Dr. Benson's work underscores the profound impact of meditation on both mental and physical health, highlighting its potential as a valuable tool in stress management and disease prevention.

Try My Simple 3-Step Guide to Meditation for Sceptics

Meditation can feel intimidating, especially if you're not sure it's for you. But the truth is, it's a simple practice anyone can try, and you don't have to believe in anything spiritual to experience its benefits. Here's an easy starter guide I recommend playing some calm music or you can download meditation music from Spotify to get you started:

Step 1: Find Your Space and Get Comfortable

Pick a quiet spot: It doesn't have to be a fancy room – just somewhere you won't be interrupted. It could be a corner of your living room, your bedroom, or even outdoors.

Sit or lie down comfortably: You don't need to sit cross-legged like a yoga goddess unless that's comfortable for you! Just sit in a chair with your feet flat on the floor or lie down. The key is to keep your body relaxed and supported.

Step 2: Focus on Your Breath

Breathe normally: There's no need to control your breath. Just let it come and go naturally.

Pay attention to your breath: Focus on how the air feels as it enters and exits your body. You might notice your chest rising and falling or the sensation of air passing through your nostrils.

When your mind wanders, gently bring it back: It's normal for thoughts to pop up. When they do, don't judge yourself – just gently bring your focus back to your breath. Think of it like a mental reset.

Step 3: Keep It Simple and Short

Start with just 3-5 minutes: You don't need to meditate for hours. Even a few minutes is enough to start feeling the benefits. As you get more comfortable, you can extend the time.

Be consistent: Try to practice daily, even if it's just for a few minutes. The key is regularity, practice not perfection.

3

Love, Loss, and Who Stayed

Cancer doesn't just affect the body, it reshapes relationships. This chapter explores the beauty of unexpected support, the heartbreak of absence, and the surprising truths that emerge.

I spent years caught in a vicious cycle of trying to please everyone around me—striving to be the perfect mother, wife, daughter, and friend. I wanted to be everything to everyone. At the same time, I expected nothing less than perfection from myself. Every day, I put an immense amount of pressure on myself to do things properly, to make everything look just so. My focus was on achieving the best possible outcomes, whether it was in my career, my family life, or personal pursuits. I believed I had to work hard, sacrifice my own needs, and keep every little detail in order. I thought that if I did everything right, I could somehow reach some ideal version of my life, one that would make me feel accomplished, loved, and accepted.

But it wasn't just the pressure from the outside world that weighed me down. The pressure from within was even heavier. I was so hard on myself, constantly believing that to achieve, I had to forgo taking care of myself. The relationship I had with myself was poor at best. I didn't love myself, and my internal dialogue reflected that in a form of self-loathing. When I looked in the mirror, I saw an image I disliked—an overweight, unattractive version of myself that I couldn't accept. I stopped dressing nicely because nothing was fitting me properly and I was always bloated. When something did actually fit me, it just didn't feel right. I wasn't comfortable in my own skin. I became disengaged with my appearance because I was the last person I took the time to care for.

My inner voice, my relationship with myself, was far too loud and harsh, constantly whispered negative thoughts. It told me that others were judging me, that they saw my imperfections, and that I wasn't good enough. I believed these thoughts. I let them control me. This was a huge issue, but at the time, I didn't know how to fix it. I didn't know how to shut down that negative self-talk, let alone start building a healthier, more loving relationship with myself. On the outside I was confident and calm.

The deeper I sank into this rut, the more I began to fantasise about escape. One day, before I was diagnosed with cancer, I remember thinking, "Wouldn't it be nice if I could just get sick and spend two weeks in the hospital? I could eat healthy food, sleep for days, and maybe even read a book." That thought, which in hindsight breaks my heart, was a clear indicator of how badly I needed rest, peace, and time for myself. I didn't know how to slow down or how to care for myself. I was trapped in a never-ending cycle of work, family, and obligations. My mind, body, and soul were all screaming for a break, but I didn't know how to stop and listen.

I had people in my life people who loved me urging me to slow down, but I couldn't do it. I didn't know how. I believed I needed to keep pushing forward—My kids needed me, my work needed me. I thought that working hard and proving myself would bring success, and that success would validate me. What I didn't realise then was that my inability to slow down, to take a step back, was not only harming me but was also preventing me from living the life I truly wanted.

The more unhappy I became, the less I worked on myself. I accepted that this was just my lot in life that I had to keep going, no matter how exhausted or overwhelmed I felt. I told myself that if I could just get to a certain point whether it was finishing a big project or reaching some milestone things would get better. But in truth, I wasn't really living in the present moment. I was constantly focused on the "if only"—if only I could get to that next goal I could finally take care of myself, then I could live the life I truly wanted.

The thing is, I didn't know where "there" was. I didn't know what that next goal would look like. I was moving aimlessly through life, hoping that by reaching some arbitrary destination, everything would somehow fall into place. But I wasn't truly living in the moment. I was wishing my life away, hoping that change would come without realising that I needed to be the one to make that change.

In my relationships with others my husband, my children, my family I struggled because I hadn't taken the time to define what I wanted. I didn't have goals for myself, let alone shared goals with my husband or family. I had secret aspirations for my career, but I didn't allow myself to pursue them because I thought everything else came first. And so, I kept pushing those dreams aside, believing that if I just kept doing more, kept sacrificing more, something better would eventually come. But it never did. I truly believed that chasing a bigger salary in my working life would improve my personal life and take the pressure off me financially. All this did was engage more stress, commitment and responsibly to my working life, which I then brought home with me and in turn this manifested into negativity, impatience and at times I felt irritable and angry.

Looking back, I realise that if I'd slowed down and truly checked in with myself, I might have made very different choices. But I was too wrapped up in my own self-imposed responsibilities to notice. It took a serious toll on my mental and emotional wellbeing.

During those years, I had no real outlet just a constant push towards the next milestone, hoping things would improve. But they never did. I ignored my own needs, turning instead to unhealthy coping mechanisms. My relationship with food became toxic. I craved sugar, salt, fat chocolate, carbs, and takeaways all for a fleeting sense of relief. But that short-lived high was always followed by guilt and promises to do better that never stuck.

Food became my way of self-medicating, an escape from the stress and dissatisfaction of living a life misaligned with who I really was. Alcohol followed a similar pattern. One glass of wine to unwind became two, sometimes more—a daily reward that slowly turned into a crutch, masking my emotional exhaustion.

I had a terrible relationship with my body. I ignored its needs and masked my discomfort with food and drink, not fully realising the damage I was doing. It wasn't just the immediate effects that concerned me—it was the long-term harm I was inflicting. Eventually, it caught up with me. Worse still, I began to see the example I was setting for my children, and it wasn't the one I wanted to leave behind.

It was a huge wake-up call when I was diagnosed with Hodgkin's lymphoma!

At the time I was officially diagnosed, I had a six month-old baby and a two-year-old. I had been so selfish in a way that would now impact those I loved the most. The illness forced me to take a hard look at my life the choices I had made, the way I had been treating myself I needed to begin the process of healing.

Having made it through my gruelling treatment and into remission, I started making changes. It wasn't an overnight shift, but more of a gradual return to who I truly was and who I wanted to become. I went back to my roots and returned to study for a full 12 months. I then decided to set up my own business at home a bold step at the time as my financial situation was extremely compromised having had time off for recovery and study, but one that brought balance back into my life. Working from home gave me more time with my family and the work-life balance I'd been desperately seeking for so long. It gave me the space to breathe, to control my environment, and to be the kind of professional I wanted to be, all while creating a life that suited the needs of my growing family.

At first, it was just a small endeavour, but the more I poured my heart into it, the more I started to see my business grow. True to my usual form I gave it my all 200% and it wasn't long before I had a loyal clientele, people who came back to me again and again, trusting me with their most cherished moments. I transformed my home set up into a thriving business. It was empowering to see something I built with my own hands begin to take off.

As the business and my family grew, I knew that personal growth had to follow suit. I couldn't give my best to others if I wasn't taking care of myself. So, I joined a boot camp group a decision that seemed daunting at first. But as I began to push myself physically, I realised how much I had been neglecting my body. I started a healthier eating plan, fuelling my body with foods that nourished me, rather than ones that left me feeling sluggish and drained. I began exercising regularly, and with each drop of sweat, I felt stronger, more capable, and more confident.

I lost weight about 15kgs, but more importantly I gained confidence. I began to feel better in my own skin, something I had been desperately longing for. This wasn't just about looking different on the outside. The transformation wasn't just physical, it was also mental and emotional. For the first time in years, I felt empowered. I felt like I was taking control of my life in a way that truly honoured myself, rather than being driven by the expectations of others.

I began to recognise the value of taking care of myself. I started to understand that my health both physical and mental was not something to be taken for granted. It wasn't something I could push aside in pursuit of more money, more success, or more approval. It had to be my priority, and for the first time in my life, I realised that I was worthy of that care and attention.

I maintained this for this for the next 12 months and kept most of the weight off.

But despite these significant changes, I learnt that transformation wasn't always linear. Unfortunately, these changes were not lasting, at least not in the way I hoped. Life had a way of throwing obstacles in my path, in the form of financial challenges and so old habits would creep back in, and I'd slip into patterns that no longer served me. As much as I wanted the changes to stick, I realised that growth and change were an ongoing process, not destinations. Some days were better than others, and that was okay.

Sadly I found myself once again seeking financial gain from the corporate world and was lured by money, company cars and fancy job titles this led to leaving behind the business I loved. I believed once again that I needed to make these changes and sacrifice my personal aspirations and needs for the greater good of my family. Striving to keep up financially and maintain a lifestyle that we were all accustomed to. I returned to my old ways of thinking and previous patterns. I once again sold myself to the belief that the quest for financial gain would make me happy. I once again allowed my health and wellbeing to be bought by the highest corporate bidder. Don't get me wrong, I loved this shit; it drove me, excited me and gave me an adrenaline rush like a junkie. I was suddenly back in the thick of it. This could have been the worst or best decision I'd ever made, in the chapters ahead you can decide if this was a pivotal positive or negative!

4

The Words No One Wants to Hear

This went on for some years. Work became my life, and my identity. I was so wrapped up in what I could achieve and what I could deliver. I had changed jobs a few times by then, each role coming with more responsibility, more corporate travel, more pressure to perform. Managing teams of people, navigating office politics, and dealing with the challenges of driving outcomes became my daily grind. It was a whirlwind of meetings, deadlines, and expectations—and in the middle of all this chaos, I was juggling a family at home.

As if that wasn't enough, by this stage I had also navigated a divorce, which brought with it a heavy emotional load, adding more financial strain to my already overburdened plate. I purchased a home by myself, a monumental decision that came with its own set of challenges and responsibilities. Now, I was a single mum with two teenagers, trying to hold it all together while navigating my own complex emotions and the practical realities of single parenthood. The positive was I was still cancer free.

To stay afloat, I returned to my home hairdressing business on Saturdays, squeezing in clients and extra hours whenever I could, but that meant even less time for my family and myself. I was now working six days a week, just trying to make ends meet, ensuring there was minimal impact on my children's lives, or so I thought. In truth, I was so caught up in making everything work—planning each day, each hour, each task—that I couldn't see the bigger picture. I wasn't spending real time with my children. I wasn't emotionally present for them. I was physically there, yes, but I was too tired, too irritable, too distracted by everything else.

Some time later, I engaged in a long-distance relationship, adding another layer of complexity to my already full life. The travel time between us was three hours one way, thus stretching myself even thinner.

Anyone reading this right now might be thinking, "Why?" And I completely understand that question, because I look back now knowing that at the time I thought this was a positive path forward into a fantastic new chapter of my life. It would in fact turn out to be one of the best choices I could have ever made as this relationship became a solid foundation for five great years and provided so much emotional and physical support in my future battle with life and illness this was meant to happen when it did..

Why did I stretch myself so thin? Why did I put myself at the bottom of the list, when I knew deep down that I wasn't happy, that I wasn't truly living? I was so consumed by making every single detail of my life fit together again! Trying so hard to manage all the moving parts, that I couldn't see what I was doing to myself. The truth is, I was completely lost in the whirlwind of responsibilities, tasks, and obligations. I had become so focused on achieving external goals success at work, providing for my family, maintaining relationships that I had lost sight of the most important thing again: myself.

During it all, I couldn't recognise that I was running on empty, that my emotional and mental well-being were being drained faster than I could replenish them. The irony was, the more I did, the less I was able to give. It was a cycle of exhaustion, frustration, and disconnection. But I couldn't see it at the time. I was too busy trying to make everything work, trying to hold it all together, that I didn't realise the damage I was causing to my own mind and body.

Looking back now, I know that I was wearing myself down piece by piece. I was no longer living; I was simply surviving, and I was doing it all again at the expense of my health, my relationships, and my happiness. I had gotten so caught up in the "doing" that I forgot about the "being." I forgot about nurturing myself mentally, emotionally, and physically. I was so busy trying to make life work for everyone else, that I had nothing left for me. And I just couldn't see it.

But that's the thing about burnout it sneaks up on you. You don't always realise it until you're deep in it, until you can't keep going any longer. And that's when the truth starts to break through the chaos, when you just know that something must change. And it sure did!

I was at work one day, and for a little while, I'd been dealing with a slight pain on the left side of my stomach, just beside my belly button. At first, I didn't think much of it just a niggle, something that I assumed would go away on its own. As a busy woman, I pushed through, thinking maybe I'd strained something or that it was just a minor discomfort that would pass.

But this day at work was different. I bent over to pick something up, and suddenly, I felt a sharp pain in my side. One of my colleagues, who was with me at the time, noticed and said, "Nic, this is not normal." He looked at me with concern and added, "You're not well. You need to go see a doctor." Normally, I would have dismissed him with my usual "I'm fine, it's nothing" response, but this time, something made me pause.

"Well, maybe I will," I said, trying to brush it off.

He insisted, "It's not that busy today. Why don't you just take off and see if you can get an appointment?"

To my surprise, I called my doctor, and miraculously, they were able to fit me in for an appointment that very day.

At the doctor's office, she felt around my stomach and said that she didn't feel anything particularly concerning. Still, she recommended I go for a CT scan just to be sure. I went that afternoon and returned two days later for the results.

"Well," she started, looking at the scan, "we don't see anything obvious, but there is some thickening in the wall of your bowel." She looked at me with a thoughtful expression and said, "I'd like to do a colonoscopy just to be sure."

I was supposed to be going on holiday the following week with my partner at the time, and I remember feeling a little unsettled by her suggestion. But without hesitation, she picked up the phone and called a colleague of hers, arranging for me to get in for an appointment and a colonoscopy, which was scheduled for Friday the same week. I had no idea what lay ahead, but I knew something wasn't right.

Friday came around and I went off to the hospital for the colonoscopy. All packed up ready for holiday leaving the next morning, I went in thinking it would be a routine colonoscopy and maybe they find something. I was not thinking they would find anything major. Anyway, I came out into recovery and woke up and the surgeon was sitting on the bed beside me, and he said to me, "Nicole, you're not going anywhere. We're admitting you. You have bowel cancer".

The frightening thing about all of this was that I had very little to go on in terms of symptoms. There was no real, consistent pain to report just a bit of niggling discomfort and the sharp pain that day in the office. Physically, everything else seemed to be functioning relatively normally. I had noticed, though, that I had lost a little weight and wasn't as hungry as I usually was. My stomach had been upset a few times, and I thought maybe I had an allergy to dairy or something else that was causing it. These were really the only signs I had, along with feeling extra tired, much more than usual. But I brushed it off as just being a busy and let's face it I was burning that candle at both ends, managing everything in my life.

So, it began. I was admitted to the ward at the hospital. The doctors explained to me that they needed to immediately send me into surgery and create a stoma into my stomach because I was just a few days away from being completely blocked, unable to go to the toilet at all. I would have been an emergency case had I have not come in for the colonoscopy when I did, and it would have been far worse.

***A stoma** is a small opening created on the outside of your body, usually in your abdomen, to help with waste removal when part of your digestive system isn't working properly. It allows waste (like stool or urine) to exit your body into a special bag or pouch attached to the stoma. The stoma is often the result of surgery, and it can be temporary or permanent, depending on the medical condition being treated. It's typically used when the colon or bladder can no longer function as usual.*

It was a shock to hear, and my mind was spinning. The surgery was scheduled right away, and they performed another colonoscopy during the process. That's when they found something even more alarming another mass of cancer at the top of my bowel.

I now had two cancers growing inside me one at the bottom of my bowel and one at the top. The surgeon told me that my bowel was riddled with polyps, and we had a serious conversation about what to do next. He laid out my options:

Option A - he could cut out the cancer and reconnect my bowel, and I could go home. But the reality was that, given the extent of the cancer, he would most likely see me again in the next four to five years.

Option B - he could remove my entire large bowel and I could live with my small bowel in operaton. The prognosis wasn't great either way

He told me I was very lucky to have come in when I did. As most of the cases he sees now, have far more severe symptoms, and the cancer has often spread to the liver and lungs. In my case, however, the cancer was still completely contained within my bowel. The relief of hearing that was momentary, as I tried to process the fact that I had cancer in two parts of my body, but the weight of it all was still very heavy.

The surgeon's words stayed with me: "You're lucky you came in when you did." But in that moment, I didn't feel lucky at all. I was completely in shock!

My mind was racing, and I didn't know what to feel or think. On this day, my youngest child was away at school camp, and we were in the middle of the COVID pandemic. I had to call my parents, trying my best not to tell them exactly what was going on. I didn't want to scare them, but I needed to ask them to bring my children to the hospital. We'd been through difficult times before, but this time, it felt different. It felt much worse, and I wasn't ready to share the full weight of what was happening over the phone.

I wanted to tell them face-to-face, to have them there with me, so that they could see the seriousness of the situation. My parents brought the children in, and that night, I delivered the news. The moment I said it out loud, it was nothing short of horrific. It was hard to comprehend that this was really happening to me, to us, *again!*

Before any surgery could begin, I had to have chemotherapy.

Before the surgery, I had to endure three months of chemotherapy. The mental instability I experienced upon receiving this news was absolute next level shattering. Just knowing I had to somehow pull on every fibre of my being to find the strength to endure this again was crushing.

Then it began every other Tuesday, I would go into the hospital for treatment, spending two nights each time while the chemotherapy drugs were administered. The effects of the treatment were brutal. Some weeks, I was too weak to leave the hospital, and on one occasion, I had to stay in for an entire two-week period because I wasn't well enough to go home.

This was all happening during the COVID-19 pandemic, so visiting hours were limited and sometimes non-existent.

I was so grateful and fortunate to have another person a close friend in my life at this time who was incredibly supportive. Taking so much pressure from my family members and partner at the time. She stayed with me through my chemo treatments at the hospital, offering company and comfort when I needed it most. My sister moved into my house, and she, along with my parents, took care of my children at home, and my partner at the time would come and go providing the most amazing support, helping to pick up the slack whilst trying to run multiple businesses in a town three hours away. I was grateful every day to those who rallied around me and stepped up when I needed them the most. When I returned home from chemo, it was incredibly taxing on everyone. The drugs they gave me especially steroids kept me feeling high and energetic for a short time, but that quickly faded. I was horrible to live with and didn't know what I wanted most of the time.

Slowly, I would crash and over the next few days, I would go from feeling okay to feeling completely drained, almost bedridden. I ended up spending most days sleeping on the couch with our faithful dog Teddy never leaving my side, unable to find any energy to do much else.

During this time, my weight dropped drastically down to about 62 kilos, which was extremely low for my height 175cms. I lost almost all of my muscle tone and was especially weak in my legs. The physical toll was immense. I became so weak I needed help just to get to and from the bathroom as I couldn't even lift myself off the toilet. My calf muscles had disappeared, and my strength was gone. I was exhausted and completely depleted.

There was a time that I remember going to the supermarket and I tried to walk through the aisles but kept losing my balance and almost fell over. My body just wasn't strong enough to hold me up anymore. I felt like an old woman, frail and fragile, struggling to stay upright. It was humbling, heartbreaking, and incredibly difficult to accept. At that moment, I felt like a completely different person, someone I didn't recognise, and it was a stark reminder of how much my body had been through.

I've always tried to find the positive in every situation, and during my treatment, I met some of the most beautiful people. There were a few ladies, and a couple of men, who were all receiving treatment around the same time some had bowel cancer, others had pancreatic cancer. We became a little community, helping each other get through the tough days. We would sit together, share cups of tea, talk about our families, and chat about our lives outside of the hospital. We supported one another through the highs and lows. Some of the people I met during that time were truly amazing. It felt like we spent a lifetime together over the three months of treatment.

Sadly, as I reflect on it now, I am not entirely sure, but I believe only one other person from that group, and I are still alive today. The rest tragically lost their battle during and after chemo. It's a bittersweet thought, and sometimes I still struggle with the knowledge of losing them, especially when I think about how I made it through while they didn't.

One of the people I connected with during treatment was a gentleman, we didn't see each other often, but when we ended up in chemo together, we chatted about our jobs and business in general. He had some great connections in the professional world, and I did too, so we exchanged LinkedIn contacts and kept in touch about business matters. Our conversations were a welcome distraction from the harsh reality of what we were both facing.

One day, I received a message from him on LinkedIn that hit me hard. He told me that his health had taken a turn for the worse and was being moved to palliative care. He shared that he likely wouldn't make it past the next four weeks. I had no idea what to say to him, struggling through tears I wrote to say goodbye letting him know he had made a difference to me in the short time we connected and it was a privellige to know him. He left behind two primary school age children and his wife. Over the next few weeks I silently carried this with me not knowing when he actually left this world. I sometimes recall him and our conversations with smile.

During that time, when people around me were struggling, there was this sense of guilt that I carried, because my prognosis was much better than theirs. It was hard to reconcile that feeling emotionally, and it made the experience even more mentally complex. Watching others fight for their lives while I was lucky enough to be progressing felt incredibly unfair.

I made it through chemotherapy, and it was time for my surgery to remove my bowel. At that point, doctors still weren't sure if I'd need to undergo another three months of chemotherapy beyond the surgery. I was nervous and unsure if my body could handle it. The uncertainty of what was to come after the operation weighed on me.

My surgeon gave me a choice whether to have a full large bowel removal (resection) and have my small bowel rejoined with no stoma or bag attached to me long term.

Or, have a full large bowel removal (resection) and live with a permanent stoma and bag never to go to the toilet again the usual way for a poo.

The ultimate decision was mine.

If I chose to be rejoined, I was told I would likely need to go to the toilet about ten times a day. Whenever I felt the urge I would have to go, meaning I'd need to always stay close to a bathroom. This option would mean I wouldn't need a bag.

The other choice was to live with a permanent stoma and ileostomy bag, which meant I would be in control of emptying and changing the bag at my discretion or when required.

I thought long and hard about it. Despite the initial shock, I decided that the stoma and Ileostomy bag option would offer me a much better quality of life. It wasn't ideal, but it gave me more freedom and control. I also learnt that the stoma could be reversed at a later date, if I decided that was the right choice for me.

An ileostomy bag *is a small pouch that is attached to an opening on your abdomen (called a stoma) created during surgery. It collects waste from the small intestine when the normal route of waste removal through the colon and rectum is no longer possible. The bag is worn* *on the outside of your body and is emptied as needed. It's used for people who have had part, or all of their colon removed or are unable to use their bowel normally due to illness or surgery.*

After that, I didn't leave the hospital for nearly two and a half weeks. During that time, I had a few different surgeries in preparation for the full removal of my bowel. It was a whirlwind of procedures, doctors, surgeons and oncologists, I was so emotional and exhausted. Finally, the day arrived for the surgery.

My choice was to proceeded with the stoma and ileostomy option, so my large bowel three and a half metres was removed in a 12-hour surgery. I came through the operation and began the long road to recovery.

When I woke up after the surgery, I waited with bated breath to hear whether I'd need more chemotherapy treatment. It was weeks later after several tests and scans and a nervous wait that I was relieved beyond words to be told I wouldn't need an additional round of twelve weeks of chemotherapy. The elation I felt was indescribable. It was a huge relief and a moment I'll never forget. I couldn't have been happier.

I am I incredibly grateful for the fantastic medical team I had around me. My doctors, my oncologist, my surgeon, and especially the nurses on my ward, I had the best support system. They gave me the care and attention I needed, and I owe my life to them. I will forever be grateful to every single person who played a part in my recovery because of these people I am able to say, "I'm still here today!"

5

Held Together by Kindness

Behind every hospital visit and every difficult day was a network of support a supportive partner, my children, family, friends, strangers, nurses, and little acts of grace and kindness that reminded me I wasn't alone.

When illness strikes, it doesn't just affect the person diagnosed; it ripples through the lives of everyone around them. I learnt that those closest to you, the ones who step up to support, are often the unsung heroes of the journey. It's not just about being there for the person going through the illness, it's about the invisible burdens carried by partners, family, and friends, and how, far too often, no one asks how *they* are doing.

My first encounter with this truth was when I was first diagnosed with cancer. I was thrust into a whirlwind of doctors, treatments, and constant uncertainty. The focus shifted entirely to my health, and the conversations became consumed with medical updates, chemotherapy appointments, and what was coming next. It was exhausting. But what often went unnoticed, and what still haunts me when I reflect on that time, is how everyone else around me were faring. The people around me, the ones who were doing everything they could to help, were quietly suffering too.

During my first diagnosis my then-husband was trying to keep things together, he became overwhelmed by the demands of this crazy new normal. He was doing his best to cope, but work became his escape. He had two young children to care for and a wife who could barely leave her bed at times. To him, focusing on work was how he could keep his own sanity. I didn't hold it against him everyone has their own way of dealing with what is going on around them. But as I lay there, too sick to get out of bed most days, I couldn't help but wish someone would have been there for him too. At the time he had me, his wife with cancer, his father being treated for cancer, and his brother newly diagnosed with cancer. All of us within a few months of each other. I can't even imagine what it must have been like to potentially face losing three people in his immediate family circle all at once. Cancer had surrounded him, and he was left to deal with it in his own thoughts, as other family members were supportive but were also pre-occupied with those other family members that were unwell.

The weight then fell on my family members who were more than willing to step in. My parents, my sister, and others took on roles that no one had expected. My mother became the primary carer of my six-month-old son and my two-year-old daughter stepping into a role I couldn't fulfill, feeding and comforting my baby boy while I could barely lift my head. Her world consisted of bottle feeds, nappies and meal preparation, cleaning and washing for all of us. My two-year-old daughter would come into my room after every chemotherapy session, her small hand reaching out to me, trying to comfort me as I lay weak in bed.

She *knew* something was wrong and needed reassurance that I was okay—even though I wasn't. Her cute and heartbreaking question was always the same and I will never forget.

She would ask, "K Mum?" "K?" looking for reassurance with a nod of her small head while she spoke.

I realised the toll this was taking on everyone around me. My illness wasn't just changing my life; it was changing theirs, too. It was hard to sit back and watch that going on around me as the person who was sick. When you're the one in the hospital bed, it's hard to think about how your partner feels, or how your children are processing it all. You're in survival mode, focusing only on getting better, unfortunately you don't even have the energy left in you to assess or acknowledge the emotional toll that the people supporting you are bearing. Much later this turned to guilt for me and a complete inability to find words to thank people as the gratitude has a magnitude much bigger than any words you can ever speak.

I can't even begin to imagine what it was like for my husband at the time we had been married around 9 years, two kids under the age of three. When I look back now and try to put myself in the same situation, I can only conclude that he must have feared losing me and of what might happen to our family. Trying to fathom how he would cope with two small children if I didn't make it through. The questions must have been swirling in his head: *Would I survive? Would I still be the person he married? Would I be able to care for our children again?* Yet we never once spoke of me "not making it" and he never spoke of his thoughts and feelings. He threw himself into work to escape, a coping mechanism that, in the long run, I came to understand. He needed time away from it all.

My parents were my rock during this time. My father came to every chemotherapy session, sat with me for hours, and never left my side. But the emotional toll of watching his daughter deteriorate, of feeling helpless as I slowly faded away with the poison being pushed through my body each session, was something he carried in silence. Each fortnight on a Monday, Dad would arrive at my front door, we would look at each other in silence, I would slip an anti-nausea tablet under my tongue, and we would get in the car. The conversation on that drive was about everything except where we were going and what was going to happen that morning. It wasn't just a battle for me who was sick it was a battle for those who loved me too. As a parent now myself thinking about having to watch one of your children go through what I did and to do what my parents did for me is beyond heartbreaking and just so emotional.

Over the past few years, I have come to realise that the people who do the supporting need just as much support, if not more, themselves. When you're sick, you're surrounded by doctors, nurses, and the medical support teams, all there to help you. But the people who are living the day-to-day realities of your illness are the people around you, they don't have that same safety net. No one asks them how they're holding up; no one checks in to see if they need someone to talk to. And in many ways, they suffer in silence.

During my second diagnosis with bowel cancer, the dynamic shifted a little. I had a very supportive partner, but this time I was in a long-distance relationship. While he did his best to support me, it wasn't easy for him. He couldn't be by my side as much as he wanted, and this created its own set of challenges. My family once again stepped up, but this time, there were other complications. My teenage children were watching me deteriorate once again, and they were scared. They had already been through this once, not that they remembered much only what they had been told in later years, and now they were facing the possibility of losing me again. The fear was palpable. Their emotions came out in many different ways some in rebellious behaviour, in anger often directed at me and others supporting our situation, and in confusion and denial not wanting to know any updates or information on my situation. Even to the point where there was just no communication at all most of the time.

To make matters worse we were in the middle of COVID-19 lockdowns and curfews. These were teenage social beings that were used to being out all the time. Friends were life and their lifeline, and they were being cut off. Also added to the mix was home schooling year 11 and 12 final high school years. My children were living an absolute teenagers nightmare and none of us knew how to help them through it. I think this was more painful for me than the physical pain I was in at the time, I felt so weak and helpless. In every other instance throughout their lives, I was always there with the answers and as a parent was always their support.

The strain on everyone was overwhelming, and I couldn't be there for them in the way I needed to be. I was lying in a hospital bed, trying to survive, yet I was still the one everyone was calling when things went wrong at home. I had no choice but try as best I could to provide phone support to the people supporting me. It was an odd position to be in, one that I don't think many people talk about, but it's a reality that countless others face in similar situations.

When you're the one fighting for your life, it's easy to forget that the people who are fighting for you need help too.

That's when I realised the true lesson of this experience: support systems are not one-sided. The caregivers, the partners, the family members they need care, too. They need to know they're not alone, that what they're going through is valid, and that it's okay to seek help. It's essential that society creates spaces for those who support the ill, spaces where they can express their emotions, seek guidance, and find community with others who are experiencing the same struggles. No one should have to carry the burden alone, not even the people carrying the burden for someone else.

These support people that love you have had their whole lives turned upside down disruption to work, social outlets and daily routines all in aid of caring for the person that is unwell. Of course, they don't mind because they love us, but it is tiring and challenging beyond belief. Often having to make difficult and personal decisions on behalf of the unwell person. This may require paying bills, dealing with upkeep of the home, parenting children and teens in their care, looking after animals and the list goes on. Until this happened to me, I had never really given much thought to my life admin and personal responsibilities, we have hundreds of them, small things we do without thought.

I was suddenly lying in a hospital bed, I was a full time employee of a company with a desk full of unfinished work and projects, I was running my hairdressing business from home with clients booked in up to eight weeks in advance, I was in the middle of refinancing my home loan to get a better deal with paperwork in progress, I had a holiday booked that I was going on the next day. I had children with sporting commitments. I had one child on school camp that was due home in the next 24hours. It is fair to say I was extremely busy. Your life outside the hospital does not stop just because you become ill.

The next day, with the help of family and friends I spent the day re arranging appointments and cancelling everything planned in my life for the foreseeable future in between doctors visiting my hospital bed and nurses attending to my medical needs.

As I reflect on the entire experience, I know that the journey wasn't just mine. It was my family's, my friends', anyone that was connected to me in anyway, everyone that knew and loved me. We all fought together. And yet, we all need to remember in the fight against illness, the unsung heroes are those who step up to support. But who's supporting them? That's the question we must answer. It's a larger question for our community going forward.

I am forever grateful to those who were there in my darkest hours, thank you will never be enough.

In this world, no one should feel like their emotions are an afterthought. They should know that they're not just helping someone get through a medical crisis they too are worthy of help and healing. It should be a world where compassion and care aren't just about the person in the hospital bed, also about the entire circle of people whose lives are forever altered by illness. People that offer to assist others and care should not end up with no one to care for them.

The solution is clear: balance and a holistic approach to care, one that nurtures everyone involved, ensuring that no one feels lost, forgotten, or unsupported.

As you grow older, you will discover that you have two hands, one for helping yourself, the other for helping others.
— **Audrey Hepburn**

6

Bag Blow Outs, Poonami's, and Laughing Anyway!

Yes, it's messy. Yes, it's mortifying. But it's also funny… well, eventually. Here is a no-holds-barred look at my new emerging life with an ostomy bag, and how humour has become my unexpected armour.

Post surgery, my new body took a lot of getting used to. As I stood looking in the mirror at my body in my underwear, I was confronted by a new me. I would never have a perfect looking torso and stomach ever again. I now had a big bag stuck on my stomach permanently. The tears rolled down my cheeks. I had to somehow make peace with this new thing.

Having an ileostomy bag attached to the skin around my stoma was a huge adjustment, both physically and mentally. It wasn't just a matter of getting used to a new physical reality; it was about navigating a whole new mindset. There were so many things to think about now. Things I never had to consider before. The constant worry that something could go wrong had me on edge.

My anxiety levels skyrocketed, and leaving the house became a daunting task. This was the new me, and somehow, I had to learn to adapt and keep moving forward. It was mentally overwhelming. I spent a lot of time in tears usually in the shower where no one could see me. I was struggling with the reality that my clothing would never fit the same again. Everything felt different; things didn't sit right, and I could see it. The new shape of my body, the bag underneath my clothes, it all made me feel like I was carrying a visible mark, a constant reminder of what had changed. At first, all I could think about was how I could hide this "imperfection" on my body.

Then came the even more challenging part: managing the bag changes. Sometimes my stoma would bleed, and at times, it almost got a nappy rash. I had to carefully move the adhesive around to allow the skin to heal, constantly managing the discomfort. And depending on the temperature, or how full the bag got, the adhesive would sometimes start to peel off, leading to leaks. I'd find myself dealing with poo soaked clothing, often in the most inconvenient situations. This bag, this constant companion, consumed my every thought and filled me with fear whenever I thought about leaving the safety of my home.

Then, there were the dreaded "bag blowouts" or "Poonamis" as they are fondly referred to amongst those of us who wear bags. Yes, I now know, sadly, there is a huge world-wide community out there full of us ostomy bag wearers, and yes we are all well versed in dealing with a leaking or blown bag!

A bag blowout happens when the adhesive between the bag and your skin lifts, causing poo to escape from underneath, sometimes silently, without any sensation. The poo would seep through my clothes without warning. It can happen at any moment, anywhere. It was not a comforting thought for me whenever I left the house. Especially going somewhere all dressed up!

When I first got home from the hospital, bag blowouts were a regular occurrence. It was embarrassing and difficult to manage. But over time, I started to understand my body better. I have figured out which foods can trigger these blowouts, and which ones were safer for me to eat. I have discovered that when you have an evening event it is easier to eat smaller amounts of food during the day to eliminate large amounts of output later in the evening. I have also discovered that early to mid-morning is when my bag is less active therefore it is the best time to exercise, swim or undertake any physical activity or be away from home at this time.

Regulating my diet became a crucial part of managing my ostomy bag and avoiding these unexpected and sometimes mortifying situations. Every day is a learning experience, trying to figure out what worked for me and what didn't, all the while adjusting to this new version of my life.

I had some funny experiences with my ostomy bag that I can now look back on and laugh about. And honestly, when I reflect on those moments, I must laugh because it was such a crazy time. There was this one instance when I was sitting on the lounge post-operation, having a conversation with my dad. Suddenly, I felt this enormous output from my bag, and I had no control over it at all. It came out at full speed, nearly blowing the bag off my stomach. There was just shit everywhere. Dad and I locked eyes, both stunned, and then, in the middle of the chaos, I started to cry. But through the tears, I also started to laugh because it was such a hopeless situation. Here I was, sitting there, covered in it, and Dad who was in front of me couldn't do a thing to help. We both started to laugh as the whole scene felt comical, but also devastatingly upsetting at the same time. All I could do was sit there in disbelief. After it finally stopped, I managed to make my way to the bathroom to clean up, but it was one of the most embarrassing and funny experiences I've had. It made me think, "What if this happens when I'm out in public?" It left me mentally exhausted and full of anxiety. I couldn't help but wonder how I was ever going to go to work again, shop or even go to a restaurant.

I can empathise with other ostomy bag wearers as some people take an exceptionally long time to get through the mental aspect of being able to get out and about away from the safety of home. It depends a lot on your body and if you can achieve regulation with food and drink to enable you to feel comfortable in social situations. This is a very personal thing and can take a long time to achieve confidence in the workplace, socially or even the simple task of going to the supermarket can be terrifying.

In my four-year ostomy experience I have found that if you let people around you know what is going on, they are a lot more empathetic and helpful if you need to suddenly leave or race to the bathroom. I have also now made it my own decision to give my employers full disclosure and have been treated with nothing but compassion and respect.

The bag can also emit gas at any time, essentially making it "fart" without any control. So yes, I can be anywhere, and unlike a normal fart, you can't control it when it happens. It's noisy, and the only good thing is that it doesn't smell because it's contained in the bag. Thankfully, now as time has passed, most of the time, it just sounds like my stomach growling from hunger, so I am able to pass it off. But occasionally it happens when I'm out and if I am around people that know me well there is much laughter and many fart jokes!

On another occasion, I was meeting a friend for a drink at a fancy hotel. I had just arrived when we sat down and ordered drinks. Suddenly, I felt something on the front of me, and when I put my hand down, I realised my bag had blown out and upon inspection of my hand it was covered in shit. Letting her know immediately I'd had bag blowout, and it was starting to seep through my clothes. She knew something was up and saw the panic on my face, I just said, "We need to get out of here." She immediately took care of everything while I rushed to cover myself with my coat and headed for the door.

As we walked at huge pace, she asked if I wanted to go to the bathroom to clean up, but I knew it was too bad to clean up in public. I said, "Let's just get in the car and go home." We ran to the car which was parked in a car park miles away and we also had to walk through a crowded shopping centre to get there. All the while my hand covered in shit, making poo jokes and laughing. The drive home was a half-hour journey, and I was covered in smelly shit. Fortunately, I had some wipes in the car, so I cleaned myself up as best I could while wrapping my coat around me. The whole experience was one I never imagined I'd go through, but there I was, heading home covered in it, trying to stay calm. With my loyal friend in the passenger seat putting up with the smell and providing humour and 100% support all the way!

Early on, I had another situation while shopping with my daughter at the supermarket. Suddenly, I felt the bag filling at an alarming rate, and I could feel the leak. I told my daughter, "We have to leave now." She had no idea what was happening and looked at me like I had lost my mind. People around you forget that you're dealing with something so personal and often invisible. It is a blessing in a way as they only see you and not the bag. In this situation I tried to quickly explain without panicking her that my bag was leaking, and her response was, "Oh, okay." She didn't fully understand the magnitude right at that moment of me just shitting all over the floor of the supermarket and for both of us the impact could have been so humiliating when I reflect back. I just told her I had to go and now!

I left her with the trolley at the checkout as we in the middle of loading groceries onto the conveyor belt for purchase. At that point, I handed my her my credit card and said, "Just pay for the groceries. I'll meet you in the car." She processed everything, still confused, and I made a run for it to the car, hoping as I went not to drop anything on the shopping centre floor. I ran with a messy poo trail dripping from my bag as I made my escape. My beautiful capable girl joined me a few minutes later with our supermarket shopping and we made our smelly way home with the windows down in the car.

It was then she realised the enormity of my new life and we both looked at each other knowing we had dodged a very embarrassing real-life situation.

Living with a bag means I have a constant fear of a blow-out/poonami in public. It's something I am faced with daily. Fortunately, I have a lot of supportive people around me who understand what I'm going through. Over time, as I've become better at managing it, people forget that I even have it. So, when it happens, it's often a shock for them. It can even happen at night if I roll the wrong way, causing the adhesive to come unstuck in bed, or if my jeans pull in a certain area, or sitting for long periods of time in clothing with a waistband can end in disaster.

I now have items that I cannot live without and carry with me when out and about or travelling, such as a waterproof mattress protector if I am sleeping over anywhere other than home. VIP poo spray has become an essential handbag item when out and about it is used to mask odours if I empty my bag in any toilet I use away from my home. One of the things that terrify me is the fact I cannot carry a spare set of clothing everywhere I go, its just not always possible. If I am in my car, I have my repair kit on standby and a spare set of clothing.

I have done a lot of work on myself to overcome fears of bag blowouts as it initially severely impacted my will to socialise and go to work.

I have used a mental rehearsal technique that I researched early on, and I still use today each time I leave the safety of my front door, I just say these two little things in my head as I go.

Positive reinforcement with myself, altering my internal dialogue:

- "I've prepared, and I know what to do."
- "It's okay if something happens. I can handle it."

Positive reinforcement/mental rehearsal can assist your brain to respond calmly and effectively.

This is the BIG question, everyone wants to know the answer to! Has this bag affected my sex life?

Yes and no, intimacy has its own set of challenges!

In my experience when you're with a partner, they must be very understanding because the bag becomes part of the dynamic. Too much moving around or a sudden grab in the wrong area could cause the adhesive to be compromised. It takes a kind caring and special person to make you feel comfortable and confident and can require a lot of patience and care for both partners.

Having intimacy with an ileostomy bag is possible, and many people with an ileostomy lead full, active sexual lives. There are a few key considerations to ensure comfort and confidence. Here are some general tips from credible sources:

Communication is key, having prior discussions with your partner about your concerns, needs, and any adjustments you might need to make. Discussing your feelings and establishing mutual understanding help to alleviate any anxieties.

It's important for both partners to be understanding of how an ostomy affects your body and how you feel about it.

Emptying the bag beforehand is essential and helps reduce the chances of leaks or discomfort, some bags allow for a fold up higher which stops it flapping around.

Emotional well-being is important as having an ileostomy may affect your body image, which can influence your confidence during intimacy. It's normal to have concerns, but it's also important to remember that your body is still capable of enjoying physical intimacy.

In conclusion, while it may require some preparation, having a fulfilling sex life after having an ileostomy is entirely possible. Experimenting with different methods to secure the bag, trying various positions, and maintaining good communication with your partner are all important steps to take.

Travel has been interesting with my ostomy bag and has certainly created some difficult situations, especially through airport security. Let's set the scene.

Over the years, as we all know a lot of drugs have been smuggled through airports and on planes using a method where the concealment is strapped to a person's body! Well on the scanning machine guess what an ostomy bag looks like? yes it can look like a concealment, so naturally, I've been pulled aside for additional screening. I've been patted down and had to explain what's going on sometimes, it feels like a major inconvenience, especially when I'm in foreign countries where people may not be as familiar with it. I've had my hand luggage pulled apart and my spare ostomy bags inspected with additional drug testing.

Unfortunately, it's becoming more common, and security have become a little more understanding in recent times, it's still embarrassing to be singled out like that. It takes a certain level of confidence to cope with those moments, and over time, I've had to build that resilience. I have developed a mindset where I just won't allow my ostomy bag to stop me doing things I really want to do. I'm not saying that I don't go through fear and anxiety in some situations I am definitely human and I think I always will have these reactions to situations, but what I have learnt is to not to allow this condition to hold me back from living a full and happy life.

Over time most forms of hidden disability, whether it's something physical or the result of an accident or illness, is becoming more accepted in society. However, the most significant challenge I've faced has been accepting it myself. Honestly, I think the people around me have been more accepting of my condition than I've been of myself. That's been the toughest mental hurdle to overcome. These days anyone that knows me well would tell you that I take pride in how I present myself, I have a love of shopping for clothing and enjoying styling and wearing nice accessories priding myself on dressing well.

After the surgery, I faced a huge challenge in trying to get back to a sense of normal, and part of that process has been accepting this "new normal" for myself.

It has taken quite some time to get there, however one of the most liberating moments in this journey has been wearing a bikini at the beach. I can't deny that people do stare, but I've learnt to put myself out there despite the discomfort. It's been a huge step toward feeling comfortable in my own skin and accepting that this is now a part of me. This is who I am now, and I need to embrace it. The ostomy bag is my little companion that will stay with me for the rest of my life, and every time I look at it, I'm reminded that I'm still here. I'm still alive, and still I rise. Without this bag, I wouldn't be here and while some days are still not easy, I've learnt to accept it as a part of my body, my journey, and my life going forward.

It may sometimes impact the way I do certain things, but it will never stop me from doing what I love. I've travelled and will continue to travel and I will still swim in the ocean because I refuse to let this ever limit me. I won't let it keep me from experiencing the world, from enjoying my passions, or from living a fulfilling life. Life with an ostomy bag is not how I envisioned my life, but it's a life I'm determined to absolutely make the most of!

Now I had my health back again and was moving into my new normal life, the coming chapters have included the lifestyle challenges and changes I have made both mentally and physically to help me stay on track.

7

When Goodbye Becomes a Kindness

Letting go of people, habits, and even parts of myself was painful but sometimes, goodbye is the bravest choice. This chapter speaks to courage, closure, and my newfound peace.

In my soul, I knew I had to leave not just a place, but a way of life. I was retreating and repeating old patterns again. I had an incredibly supportive partner and a new home environment; however, our relationship was built with the pre cancer me with the lifestyle and patterns that I was living prior to cancer. The constant cycle of drinking, unhealthy eating, and emotional instability was slowly eroding who I was. I was no longer reacting to life with clarity or calm. I was trying so hard to rebuild a new life with a country location, new home, I was exercising to build strength and trying find a new job that would feed my soul and create an income to contribute to my new life.

My environment was saturated with stress, and sleep came in short, broken bursts. The atmosphere around me was so tense, it felt like even rest had become impossible. I had no space of my own to escape to when I needed to recalibrate. I was physically drained, emotionally spent, and somewhere deep inside, I knew I couldn't carry on like that.

The energy in the house and around me was always tense and high the only time I relaxed was with a glass of wine at the end of the day. I had done my meditation teaching course and was struggling to find headspace and physical space to enjoy my practice.

Spirituality and meditation were not taken seriously by those around me, so I only found time when I was alone, and this was not often. I couldn't breathe there was no space for me. No calm quiet little space that was mine and mine alone to work on me and where my life was heading now beyond my illness. I knew in my heart and soul I needed a reset and I guess I was just hoping I could count on my new environment and the people around me at the time to walk this new line alongside me.

What I did discover in the time I was waiting for this to happen was you cannot stay in the same environment and expect change to evolve, or people to change for you and if you change you cannot expect that they will understand and support the change within you. Nor continue to travel this future path with you. Sometimes what must happen then needs to happen to you alone.

I was changing and everyday slowly but surely, I was feeling like I did not belong in the same environment that once made me feel so loved, respected and happy. I started to understand that if I did not find the strength to make changes that I would surely end up unwell again and possibly die this time.

I had my children and family to live for and all the things I hadn't seen and done. I wanted to travel and explore. My priorities had changed dramatically including my want to live with less material things, striving to make money became a lower priority, I realised this life is short and I wanted things, big things I wanted a big full life and to achieve all the things I had not yet accomplished. I wanted experiences and creativity I didn't even know exactly what some of these things were yet. I just knew I was still here on this planet for a reason, and I had to find my true purpose, my why.

I was left wondering how all of this could be so clear in my head, yet I had become someone that the people around me did not understand. I know now why people don't understand me because I am unique and they were my thoughts and my feelings no one else's, these came as a direct result of going through a painful life altering experience.

I was people pleasing afraid to speak my truth in fear of hurting everyone around me. The person I was hurting the most by not doing this was myself. I was repeating old patterns, just living each day as the person everyone wanted me to be and not who I had now become. This in turn became a pressure cooker for my relationship until one night it happened. I could feel it slowly rising over the days prior coursing through my body and soul until it finally exploded I was suffocating I couldn't breathe I had to run from it all.

I was in full fight or flight, my heart was pounding, my eyes and cheeks stung with the tears, horrible words were exchanged, and I drove away into the night. I couldn't believe it had happened it was like being in a bad dream. Yet the pull to elsewhere was to be so incredibly strong and for once I was listening to my own feelings' thoughts and needs.

Terrified of what lay ahead as I drove and drove, I soon felt a calm that passed over me. There were so many emotions attached to this calm. I felt freedom, I felt sadness and loss leaving behind these things and people I loved so much. I felt fear leaving behind all the comfortable and familiar surroundings.

Even with all this racing through my head, it was at that moment I knew I was never going back. My five year relationship was over, some friendships were over, my current home life was over, and any future plans that involved all of this were now over.

Not only did I leave people behind, I left a lot of possessions behind also. The need for less in my life has been pivotal, removing material things around me has been challenging and cleansing. I had let go of physical things that no longer serve me. Possessions mean so much less to me than ever before.

The value that I now place on the "stuff" we all have and accumulate over so long is very minimal. It has not always been this way. I was the queen of stuff when it came to the latest decorator cushions or a new lounge suite, not to mention the latest electrical appliance yes, the steam iron or food processor had to be the latest and greatest. Stuff is not just household items it includes the amount of clothing, shoes and handbags I owned back then, and it was seriously next level ridiculous, at one count I owned 150 pairs of shoes. I think back now and my relationship with stuff was status, it symbolises success, well that's what my little friend (internal dialogue was telling me). I so fixated on what everybody thinks instead of what I could afford or really needed in my home and wardrobe. I used to think that I needed a house full of things to make me happy.

I now understand that all these purchases were filling a void, a dopamine release, when you purchase something new it can trigger the brain to release dopamine, a "feel-good" thing in your brain, in turn creating a sense of reward or pleasure.

Yes I still have possessions and occasionally love a good shoe purchase, I try now to only have things that mean the world to me things that were gifts or photos, some things from my childhood, things from my children, things that have memories attached to them all of these things are significant.

My relationship with "stuff" has changed dramatically I have lost attachment to most material things and now only surround myself with things that have meaning are sentimental or a functional purpose and are useful.

All the beautiful, shiny objects we surround ourselves with hold energy and when there is a lot of things surrounding you in your home, office or general space all that energy can influence you consciously or unconsciously. Creating a feeling of chaos and influence how grounded you are.

Clearing out and learning to live without a lot of stuff has been a big part of my healing process. It has been healing in the way it has allowed me to free myself of obligational attachment.

Obligational attachment to items makes you feel a sense of duty or responsibility to keep and maintain possessions, often driven by guilt, sentimental value, or keeping items due to the expectations of others.

I have had some hard lessons that have taken time to overcome and some that resurface on occasion after all we are human not perfect. You cannot run away from thoughts and feelings; they are with you wherever you go. You can however change your external environment enabling you space to tackle those thoughts, feelings and emotions.

My need for space and solitude grew the longer I was in a calm environment, the days passed, and I grew the strength and much courage it took to be able to tell people around me some quite close that I was disappearing for a while. This was not met with understanding it was met with first concern then anger and misunderstanding. At this point I was shutting down and completely depleted of energy to even try and spend time explaining. Absolute exhaustion was setting in and I was almost mentally incapable of having intense conversations. I did know and believe at that time I would emerge a butterfly on the other side and when I did the people that were supposed to continue the journey with me would still be there.

I just needed to be able to breathe spend time in reflection and work on me. I needed to be far from all the things that brought me to the point of needing to run and change. I had no idea where I was heading and how I was going to achieve what was required to rebuild my life, all I knew was it needed to be different in so many ways.

It was a profound experience when I disappeared and stopped chasing people, stopped calling, stopped trying to fit in with them, I found they in return made no effort to seek me out. It was just the sound of silence and it felt so good, silence was what I craved and needed it felt comfortable calm like a happy homecoming in my soul. This was a major learning for me also. While others made minimal contact and respected my request for space and healing. Some still checking in and letting me know they were there should I need anything. I was finally in a respected space. The healing had permission to begin.

I also experienced some of the most profound and everlasting solid support from family and friends in my life during this period. This was true emotional and physical support. Just pure love and caring. I believe that the universe provides just what you need when you need it and I have absolute faith in this after what came next.

It came to me in the form of an offer through a friendship so aligned that was my absolute true north, so pivotal in my healing I could never have known how this would reshape, heal and provide food for my soul.

A month of house and dog sitting time out by the ocean. Looking after two beautiful canine personalities, that sat with me walked with me cuddled with me and healed with me, they were the best company I could have ever asked for. As I started out on this little adventure with my two doggie companions by the sea, I began to feel like this was my place as I have always been an ocean lover and have talked for years about living near the beach. Completely unaware of how important this would be in my life ahead and how it would reshape my future realigning me mind, body and soul.

Four weeks alone, and I couldn't leave. I began to finally get to know myself again.

All these experiences with people and the human behaviour around me made me take a closer look at myself and my behaviour. I realised it then that I had been trying so damn hard to fit into other people's lives by maintaining constant contact which added to the exhaustion and stress that I spoke of in my earlier chapters. I had been slapped in the face with the cold hard realisation that I just wasn't that important to them. This was not something I got over quickly as like any loss in life you need to grieve, and it takes time. I had to give myself time and permission to grieve my old life, the people left behind, things I enjoyed doing and places that were part of my world for so long.

When you choose yourself and take a hardline to work on you it upsets some of the people around you. They find it hard to deal with the fact your behaviour has changed, and you are no longer saying yes to their requests, questions, expectations of you and your reactions are different towards them in some situations. It is also necessary to put space between you and others to achieve the best results and this hits hard for some are not used to having you further away or less accessible. It gets hard for a long while and you feel like you are letting others down, the irony is that by saying yes and not choosing yourself you are letting you down.

Some will not cope with the change in you and will choose to leave or move away from you as they don't understand, often taking it personally. Understanding that these are learnt patterns from childhood we are taught not to upset anyone, keep the peace and everyone will be happy. It is human nature we like to be liked and most of us don't like to be disliked.

My new favourite saying to myself is that I won't always be everyone's cup of tea, and it's alright if I am not liked so long as I am being my true authentic self.

It is impossible to please everyone all of the time and so stressful trying to maintain this, in fact, there will definitely be some that will not like this book or me after reading it, but I have learnt to be okay with this.

There were a lot of people that didn't like my decision to choose me and essentially save myself. If I had continued to try and please all of them I may not be here today healthy, extremely happy and well. I write this book and share all of my experiences in hope that this insight may inspire others to make healthy changes, put themselves first and take good care of their mind body and soul. The turning point for myself was now knowing I had this and I could do it alone!

8

Tired but Trying

Fatigue became a companion I never asked for. Here, I unpack the truth behind the exhaustion and why being tired is not the same as giving up or being lazy.

Recently, I've come to realise that tiredness doesn't equal laziness. And more importantly, it's essential to allow yourself to rest, recharge, and heal. This chapter is about how I learnt that, and how the process of truly understanding my own tiredness changed my life.

For as long as I can remember, I used to equate tiredness with laziness. If I was resting, I believed it meant I was being lazy. If I wasn't working, if I wasn't moving, if I wasn't being "productive", I thought I was failing in some way. If I needed to lie down, if I had to stop and take a break, then surely, I was just being lazy, right? I carried that belief with me for most of my life, a quiet undercurrent that made me push through exhaustion rather than pause to rest.

Having had the courage to leave and return to a safe retreat with family initially before my beach sabbatical, it was only then that I realised just how exhausted I was, not just physically, but mentally and emotionally. It wasn't that I was tired from the usual demands of daily life. It was something much deeper something I couldn't quite articulate at the time but knew I had to confront.

My entire being felt depleted. It was as if my soul had been drained, leaving me hollow and constantly fatigued. I had spent so long in a state of exhaustion, giving pieces of myself away to others, to responsibilities, to life, and the big fight to survive illness I didn't even recognise how much energy I had lost.

I'm not talking about the tiredness you feel after a busy day at work or an intense workout. This was a different kind of tiredness. It wasn't something that could be solved by a night of sleep or a quick break. It was a deeper exhaustion mental, emotional, and physical. Everything felt like it took more effort than it should have. And I found myself getting caught in the trap of thinking, *if I just push through, I'll be fine*. But I wasn't fine. It took me some time to realise that it was okay to not be fine, to not feel like I had to be constantly going.

Restful Doing:

Post treatment for cancer I had begun to use colouring in to switch off my brain and relax by only thinking about the colours and patterns, during this mindful meditative practice I would colour in mandalas and pictures from colouring books, eventually using colour and creating a few canvas art pieces. I found this was deeply therapeutic with the knowledge I wasn't racing off to the next appointment, I was finally giving myself permission to heal creatively.

Try this meditative mindful practice to calm your mind and give you time out:

Start with colouring books, concentrate on the intricate patterns and detailed designs that demanded your full attention.

Choose mandalas or repeat patterns to start with, as the circular, or symmetrical patterns feel calm and structured.

Try listening to meditation music whilst doing this activity it will aid concentration and calm.

As you colour, note your quietened mind.

Allow other thoughts to come in and gently send them away.

The only thing right now should be the act of colouring.

Allow the rhythm of filling in spaces with different colours to become a form of mindfulness.

Just be present with the colours and the patterns.

Eventually, I expanded beyond the pages of colouring books and began creating my own art. I started using colour on a canvas, with each stroke of the brush or pencil, it wasn't about creating something "perfect." It was about the freedom to express myself through colour, to let my emotions flow out in ways words couldn't capture.

One of the most restful parts of this creative journey came when I spent time with my mum in her art studio. Being surrounded by her art and the peaceful environment of the studio felt like a sanctuary. The act of creating art, whether it was through the intricate designs of mandalas or the abstract strokes on a canvas, it became an intimate ritual of self-care. The space was full of quiet inspiration, it is difficult to explain it was just something I needed to do to disconnect and to create space to my own healing process. It was very therapeutic and place where I didn't feel time constraints or exhaustion as I could come and go when I pleased".

> *"Art therapy can assist individuals in expressing their feelings, reducing stress, and improving mental health by fostering self-reflection and emotional processing through creative means."*
> **— Australian Association of Art Therapists, 2021**

The first few days after I returned to Melbourne felt like a blur. I couldn't muster up the energy to do much of anything. I'd find myself stuck in cycles of overthinking and worrying about everything I wasn't doing, even as my body screamed out for rest.

Slowly, over time, I began to recognise what I needed to truly heal. I needed to give myself permission to rest. I needed to recharge, not just my body, but my mind and soul. This process was slow.

One of the things that helped me begin this healing process was meditation as I have referred to in previous chapters it was pivotal in my recovery and reset. It became my refuge. I would wake up early in the mornings, sit in silence, and allow my thoughts to calm down. The physical act of stillness brought me a sense of relief that I had been craving for so long. After meditating, I would go for walks, breathing in the fresh air and grounding myself in nature. It sounds simple, but it was life altering and calm. Walking and breathing slowly, without the rush of a to-do list hanging over my head, helped me reconnect with my body. I started to feel less frantic inside, less overwhelmed by the noise in my head. I also joined the local gym and began slowly working on my muscle strength always listening to calm music or inspirational podcasts while doing my workout.

I knew that the physical aspect of rest was just as crucial to my overall wellbeing. I had been neglecting my need for rest for far too long. Before, I'd push myself to stay up late, believing that the more hours I worked, the more I could accomplish. Now I began to establish a very strict routine as I made the conscious decision to prioritise sleep and rest. I started going to bed early, sometimes as early as 8:00 or 9:00 p.m. with the allowance to read for half an hour, then I would listen to a sleep meditation or the recorded sound of the ocean with waves lapping onto the beach, sending me slowly off to sleep. Ensuring I got the full 8-9 hours of sleep to replenish my body. I had to teach myself that rest wasn't a luxury it was a necessity. It was through this daily ritual of rest and recovery that I started to feel a shift.

Something I still do every night is sleep with the curtains open. This allows my body to naturally awake the next day with a brand-new sunrise and light slowly and softly drifting into the room. It is such a beautiful way to wake from sleep and welcome a new day. A far cry from the jolting alarm, this new form of waking still allows enough time to complete a meditation and manifestation all before my beloved coffee.

I realise now how long and difficult this process was. It wasn't a quick fix. I spent days, and weeks, simply recharging. And even though I felt guilty at times for not being as "productive" as I had been before, I started to understand that this wasn't laziness. This was self-care and a vital step in healing.

Adding to my exhaustion was my diabetes diagnosis, which complicated the situation. After being diagnosed with diabetes, I was forced to rethink how I fuelled my body. Fortunately, I had the professional guidance from a fantastic dietician who has worked with me to establish food choices that work with all of my conditions. I must eat to manage my diabetes, and that means making some difficult dietary choices that work for my stoma / ileostomy as well. I must be mindful of the foods I consume in order to manage my stoma output. It is and always will be a constant balancing act, one that is often frustrating and challenging. I cannot just eat whatever I want to. Some foods that are a great choice for my diabetes are not a great choice and cause problems with my stoma, and vice versa.

The foods I eat for diabetes can impact my level of energy and tiredness.

If type 2 diabetes is left unmanaged, it can lead to serious health complications affecting various parts of the body. These include heart disease, stroke, kidney disease, eye problems, nerve damage, and foot ulcers.

The 2021 Australian Quality Clinical Audit encompassed both type 1 and type 2 diabetes, as it is part of the broader Australian National Diabetes Audit) . Therefore, the reported statistics—10% experiencing myocardial infarction (heart attack), 5.4% having a stroke, and 4% developing end-stage kidney disease within the past year—apply to adults with either type of diabetes.

These figures underscore the heightened risk of cardiovascular and renal complications in individuals with diabetes, irrespective of type. It's important to note that the AQCA data are based on clinical audits and may not represent the broader population of people with diabetes.

According to the 2023 Snapshot of Diabetes in Australia by Diabetes Australia, approximately one-third of Australians living with type 2 diabetes report experiencing some form of cardiovascular disease. This condition can lead to fatigue and reduced energy levels, affecting daily activities and overall quality of life.

In Australia, approximately 125 people are newly diagnosed with type 2 diabetes each day.

*JAMA Oncology study found that the incidence of diabetes among cancer survivors was approximately **six times higher** than in people without cancer, with the greatest risk occurring within two years post-treatment. This elevated risk is thought to stem largely from treatment-related factors—such as glucocorticoids, weight changes, and chemotherapy-related metabolic disruptions—which disturb glycaemic control during and beyond treatment.*

For a while, I felt trapped in this cycle of trial and error, constantly trying to find a solution that worked for both my conditions. There were days when I felt like I was failing, when the balance seemed impossible to find. But eventually, I did find it. I learnt which foods worked best for both my body and my health conditions, and slowly, I began to feel more energetic and more in control. My meals became a concise effort of selfcare, and I began to appreciate the nourishment and energy fuel I was giving my body.

In addition to healthy eating, I found that the process of navigating my body's medical needs while eating out was another challenge. I love going to restaurants and cafes, and I am determined to not have any of these conditions or changes to my life impact the things I love to do.

Dining out with diabetes and a stoma/ileostomy means that I must be extra careful. At first, I would apologise for needing to adjust the menu or request substitutions and changes to the menu offerings. I felt embarrassed and like I was inconveniencing the waiter and chef or worse making the experience uncomfortable for those joining me at the table. Over time, I stopped apologising. I learnt how to navigate the menu quietly, how to order what I needed without drawing attention to myself. I no longer feel like a burden. Instead, I feel confident and accept the new version of me. I have figured out a way to still enjoy life, to still find joy in the small things like eating out and sharing a meal with others, while honouring my body's needs.

All of this rest, self-care, mindful eating was part of a larger lesson I had to learn that tiredness is not laziness. It's a signal from your body, a call to stop, to pause, and to rest. We live in a world that values productivity above all else, where the constant hustle is celebrated, and rest is often seen as a sign of weakness. In my life, I've come to understand that this isn't true. Rest isn't a sign of laziness; it's an act of self-respect. It's a recognition that your body and mind need time to heal, to recover, and to restore.

Now, when I feel tired, I listen. I no longer berate myself for needing rest. I know that taking the time to recharge is just as important as the work I do, if not more so. Because without proper rest, without giving yourself the space to heal, you cannot truly be at your best. Tiredness, after all, is just the body's way of telling you it's time to stop. And when you finally stop, listen and rest, you allow yourself the opportunity to come back stronger, more energised, and ready to face whatever comes next.

In the end, embracing rest has been one of the most powerful changes I've made in my life. It has taught me that being kind to yourself, taking the time to heal, and giving your body the care it needs isn't laziness. It's a form of strength a recognition of your humanity and the need to recharge. We all deserve that. And sometimes, it's the most important thing we can do for ourselves.

In the next chapter it will become clearer as I explain how changing my environment has had a huge impact on my healing and life reset.

9

The Gift Alone Without Being Lonely

Solitude, that I once feared, became sacred. This chapter is a quiet celebration of stillness, self-discovery, and finding comfort in my own company during the sun of summer through to a long winter.

As I mentioned back in chapter 7, after having the the courage to leave so much behind, I spent a month of house and dog sitting some time out by the ocean, this turned into a permanent new home and where I've been ever since it is here that I have learnt all of my lessons on being okay with being alone.

Solitude is often considered an uncomfortable state by many. It's associated with isolation, loneliness, or even boredom. But I have learnt the true power of solitude when it unexpectedly became the greatest gift I could receive. I had no idea how spending time with myself would transform my life in profound ways. Sometimes, the most unexpected gifts are the ones we don't recognise at first.

It all started with a simple invitation from friends who asked if I would house-sit and dog-sit for them at their beach house in a small seaside town near Melbourne. The idea sounded great, and it was summertime taking care of their two large dogs while enjoying a calm beach environment. I needed a break, looking for some peace and space to reconnect with myself. Little did I know that this would mark the beginning of significant change and self-discovery.

When I agreed to house-sit for them, I was simply looking for a chance to have some quiet time and a four-week working holiday. I didn't fully comprehend how much this time would change me. The dogs, though large and strong, quickly became my companions. Each day, as I walked them along the beach, they seemed to enjoy being the centre of my world and enjoyed the connection, even if it was just with nature and the simple joys of the world around us. We soon established a daily routine together. The beach, with its large expanse and crashing waves, became a sanctuary where I could just *be*.

There's something about the ocean that has always called to me. I don't just mean its beauty, though that alone is breathtaking. There is a rhythm to the waves, a pull in the tides that speaks to something deeper within. And during this quiet time, I began to reconnect with myself. Each morning, I would wake early to catch the sunrise, a ritual that slowly started to fill me with peace and purpose. I would take long walks with the dogs, listening to the sound of the waves crashing against the sand, breathing in the salty air, and feeling the sand between my toes. For the first time in a long while, I didn't feel the need to rush anywhere or be anyone other than who I was in that moment.

As the weeks passed, I became more involved in the local community. I joined a yoga class and participated in a sunrise connection group, where people gathered on the beach to connect with themselves and each other before the world awoke. It was there that I was asked to host a meditation session, an invitation that would prove to be another major milestone in my journey. Sharing my practice with others not only deepened my connection to the stillness within me, but it also gave me a sense of purpose and belonging in this small town.

I noticed something else that was happening within me: the more time I spent alone, the more I understood who I truly was. There were no distractions, no busy schedules, no constant demands on my attention. It was just me, the dogs, the ocean, and my thoughts. And in that solitude, I discovered parts of myself I hadn't realised were there. Some were comforting, others more challenging. But all of them were necessary for my growth.

In this time of solitude, I found myself reading books, meditating, and journaling, all of which fed my soul. I didn't feel the pressure to entertain myself with television or social media. Instead, I created space for reflection, for deep thinking, for *being* rather than doing. I began to embrace the beauty of stillness and the profound lessons that came with it.

But this journey wasn't just about quiet reflection. It was about transformation. About shifting my mindset and allowing new possibilities to enter my life. Really working out and defining what it was I wanted for me. One night, as I lay in bed, I began manifesting, repeating affirmations that resonated deeply with me. I manifested abundance, health, happiness for my now adult children, for travel and new experiences. I did this for ten minutes each night, playing beautiful meditation music as I affirmed the changes I desired. Slowly, but surely, things began to shift.

One of my affirmations was that I would write my book, and not long after, I began working on this manuscript. Another affirmation was that I would find a beautiful home by the ocean, and I realised that I had already found it the very beach where I was staying.

The images from my vision board I had created a year earlier, began to come to life before my eyes. On that board were pictures of people practicing yoga by the beach, a house by the ocean, and money flowing easily to me from different sources. It was all happening; in ways I hadn't anticipated.

Looking back, I realise how significant this experience was. It wasn't just about living by the beach or finding a new place to call home. It was about reconnecting with myself alone, shedding the guilt and baggage I had carried for years, and finding self-compassion. I realised how much I had been holding onto past mistakes, regrets, and self-doubt. But solitude gave me the space to forgive myself, to heal, and to love myself fully, imperfections and all. I discovered that to love others, I had to first start loving me; all of me, the good bits and the bad, including all my misgivings.

There was a moment about halfway through my third week that I realised I didn't want to leave this beautiful enviroment. The peace, the clarity, and the sense of belonging was too strong this place had captured me I couldn't walk away. It wasn't just a vacation or a temporary escape; it had become my life and felt so right. I talked to my friends, and they gave me the greatest gift of all: permission to stay longer. That simple, kind gesture shifted my life forever. It was then that I decided I would make this place my home.

What followed was a gradual but powerful process of reinvention. I found a part-time job in the community, which provided financial stability while also allowing me to pursue my passions. I became more deeply connected to the environment and people around me, making new friends and building relationships that nourished my soul. I explored creative endeavours and embraced a lifestyle that prioritised mental health, wellness, and growth.

Throughout this period, I continued to manifest new opportunities and goals. I manifested success for my book, and I saw it start to materialise in ways I could never have imagined. I also manifested financial freedom, which has now allowed me to let go of huge financial burden, thus enabling me to travel and experience more of what life has to offer. The process of manifestation became a powerful tool for shaping my reality, and I began to understand that everything I needed was already within me.

One of the most sobering aspects of my journey has been the recognition of how important it is to create your own happiness. It's not something that happens by accident or something you find in an external place. It's something you cultivate from within, and the more I embraced this truth, the more I began to feel at peace with my life. I am now in my fifties, and for the first time in a long while, I can honestly say that I am the happiest I've ever been. I have a healthy body, a peaceful mind, and a heart full of love for myself, the people around me and the life I've built.

The beach, the ocean, and the surrounding community have become integral parts of my identity. I now walk on the beach every day, swim in the cold ocean waters regularly, and enjoy the stillness that nature offers. The simple joys of life like walking the dogs on the beach, feeling the sand between my toes, and listening to the waves have become my greatest sources of peace. I've learnt to live mindfully, to fully experience the present moment without rushing or taking anything for granted.

What's fascinating is how the beach changes every single day. The tides shift, the sand forms new patterns, and the sea life changes with each passing day. And yet, no two days are the same. This mirrors my own journey a continuous evolution, where every moment brings something new, something unexpected. I've learnt to appreciate the beauty in that fluidity, knowing that life is not static, change is inevitable.

I often reflect on the people who come to this town, the tourists who arrive with the weight of their busy lives, carrying stress and worry in their every step. I see them walking fast, heads down, glued to their phones, missing the magic of the beach, the beauty of the waves, the soothing rhythm of the ocean. It reminds me of how easy it is to be distracted, to forget to *be* present.

But then there are the people, the ones who have chosen this life, the ones who live with conscious intention. They move slowly, with awareness, greeting the world around them with kindness. They're the ones who swim in the ocean every morning, no matter the season. They understand the balance between work and self-care, and they live with a sense of purpose and fulfillment.

These are the people I now surround myself with. They've become my community, my support system, and my inspiration. And through them, I've learnt that happiness is not something you find it's something you create. I've also realised that when you take the time to be still, to connect with yourself, and to listen to your heart, you can unlock a life full of joy, peace, and endless possibilities.

As I write this chapter, I sit here looking out at the ocean, coffee in hand feeling its pull on my soul. This place has become my sanctuary, my home. And for the first time in my life, I can say that I've found the balance I've been searching for. If this new improved chapter of my life has taught me anything, it's this: If you're given the opportunity to step into the unknown, to embrace solitude, don't hesitate. Sometimes, the best gift you can give yourself is the gift of space to rediscover who you truly are.

And when you do, you'll be amazed at the life that unfolds.

"Take a good look at the things that are in your power, and those which are not. You will see that the latter are not worth your attention, and that what belongs to you is enough for a tranquil life. Do not seek the tranquillity that comes from external things, but the one that comes from within, from your own thoughts. Those who do not understand this, who seek fulfillment in distractions or in the opinions of others, will never find peace. But when you turn inward and focus on your own nature, which is in harmony with the universe, you will find the deepest sense of calm, free from the noise of the world."
— Marcus Aurelius, Meditations, Book 6, Section 30

10

Loving Myself Outloud

I learnt to show up for myself confronting scars, stoma, and all. A fierce and honest reckoning with my self-worth, body image, and why self-love isn't selfish it is allowed and it's essential.

Today, I understand that living in the moment, taking care of myself, and embracing self-love are not optional. They are essential. I have come to learn that the relationship I have with myself sets the tone for every other relationship in my life. Self-love is the foundation on which I can build every connection, every interaction, and every moment of my existence. I have learnt, sometimes the hard way, that if I do not nurture myself, I cannot effectively nurture others. If I do not show up for myself, I will not be able to show up for those I care about in the way they deserve.

When I look in the mirror now, I see someone I love. I look at the lines on my face and realise that every wrinkle, every mark, and every imperfection tell a story of the life I've lived and the lessons I've learnt. Those marks are not signs of weakness or failure; they are signs of growth, resilience, and the beautiful journey I am on. I completely accept this version of myself now. I love myself for who I am, not for the way others may see me, but for the person I have become.

One of the most powerful ways I have learnt to embrace self-love is through taking care of my body. For years, I did not realise how much I was neglecting my physical health. I would put harmful food into my body without thinking twice. I did not always treat my body with the respect and care it deserved. I would drink alcohol excessively, overindulge in unhealthy foods, and not get enough rest. But over time, I have come to realise that my body is the vessel that carries me through life, and this body deserves to be treated with kindness and respect.

Today, I nourish my body with wholesome food, I exercise regularly, use a combination of meditation, mindfulness, and manifestation. I feed my brain with knowledge by reading books, travel experiences and talking to people learning about their experiences and lives. Most importantly making sure to get enough rest. I no longer punish myself with unhealthy habits. Instead, I honour my body with everything it needs to stay strong and healthy. My belief is that true self-love starts with self-care taking the time to nourish and protect my physical well-being. When I treat my body with respect, I feel more energised, more alive, and more capable of facing the challenges that come my way.

One of the most significant lessons learnt on my journey toward self-love is the importance of setting boundaries. I used to think that being kind to others meant putting everyone else's needs before my own. I would say yes to things I did not want to do, and I would stretch myself so thin trying to please everyone around me. But over time, I have realised that this was depleting my energy mentally, emotionally, and physically.

Setting boundaries is not selfish; it is necessary for self-preservation. I have learnt to say *no* when I need to, to protect my time and energy, and to prioritise my own well-being. This has been a game-changer in how I approach relationships, both with myself and others.

Boundaries are the invisible lines that define what is acceptable and what is not in my life. They help me safeguard my mental and emotional health, and they prevent me from overcommitting or taking on responsibilities that are not mine to bear.

When boundaries are put in place remember, it becomes possible to create a space where we can be our best self. I try extremely hard to not let the opinions or judgments of others affect how I feel about myself. (Sometimes still a work in progress I am by no means perfect).

This is an extremely hard one as I am human, and it is human nature to want to be liked. One of the ways to help this is assessing who you choose to spend time with, I no longer surround myself with people who make me feel inadequate, who drain my energy, or criticise me for simply being myself. Instead, I choose to spend time with those who uplift me, encourage me, and who respect my boundaries.

Being self-aware has been another crucial aspect of embracing self-love. I have become more mindful of my thoughts, my feelings, and my actions. I was always someone that had an opinion and at times felt the need to share everything. I now listen more and contribute less, not because I don't want to have a voice it is because I want to make sure that my contributions have more value. I know that thoughts can become what you create. If I am constantly filled with negative self-talk or doubts, that energy will manifest in my life. On the other hand, if I focus on the positive and surround myself with affirmations of love and acceptance, I can shift my entire mindset.

This is a little mantra that sits on the fridge in my home, handwritten on a yellow post it note:

- What you think you create
- What you feel you attract
- What you imagine you become

Often in conversations with those I love when things get hard, I refer to these 3 lines above.

Now, I am much more intentional about the thoughts I allow into my head. I choose to surround myself with positivity and self-compassion. I am mindful of my internal dialogue and work every day to treat myself with the same kindness that I would offer to a loved one.

I practice mindfulness daily a simple act of walking in the morning has become a sacred ritual for me. As I step outside, I take a deep breath and embrace the world around me. I focus on the birds in the trees, the sound of my footsteps on the pavement, and the beauty of the day unfolding. This small act of mindfulness helps me connect with the present moment and sets the tone for the day ahead. I no longer rush through my mornings, feeling stressed or anxious. I take the time to centre myself and prepare mentally for the day. I often do a meditation in bed before getting up for the day. Another one of my routines is listening to a motivational or manifesting podcast whilst I work out at the gym instead of music.

I have also learnt that self-love means carving out time for myself. Life is busy. There's always something to do, someone to take care of, the house needs to be cleaned, dishes, meals to prepare or washing to be done!

To be honest these were some of the things I found the hardest to let go of. I realised that it was giving me purpose and a strange sense of my having my life under control. Learning these things need to be done but can be left if you need time for yourself has been necessary, those tasks will still be there, I know that is stating the obvious but I have found it extremely hard to detach from needing to have all my ducks in a row before I can have time for me.

I challenge you to sit on the couch and look at a full basket of washing that needs folding while reading a book. For most of us this is insanely hard.

It was like a child letting go of their security blanket and has taken me quite some time to master.

I do know I cannot pour from an empty cup, and for me now an empty cup could result in more illness. I have realised that if I do not prioritise self-care and downtime, I'll burn out.

I make it a point to schedule time for activities that bring me joy and relaxation. Sometimes, that means spending a Sunday afternoon on the couch with an enjoyable book or a coffee in bed some mornings to slow life down a bit. Something this simple would have previously created feelings of guilt or would have seemed impossible in the past. I used to think I did not have time to rest, that there was always something more important to do. But now, I realise that rest, recharging, and reconnecting with myself are just as important as productivity.

Taking walks on the beach has become another act of selflove. Always grateful for where I am now. These walks give me the space to clear my mind, breathe in the fresh air, and reflect on my life. It is now in these beautiful moments of stillness that I feel most connected to myself and to the world.

I have had to learn to empower others to find their own answers, especially my children instead of always being the one to fix things for them. I have had to let go of the need to be everyone's saviour, to stop carrying everyone's burdens, and to trust that the people I love can find their own way. I have learnt that I do not need to sacrifice my own well-being to make others feel better. When I choose to invest in myself, I am not taking away from anyone else. Instead, I am giving myself the strength and energy to be the best version of myself, which benefits everyone around me.

I have had people in my life who did not understand my journey toward self-love. They wanted me to be the person I was before, the person who would drop everything for them, who would sacrifice my own needs to please others. I want you to understand when reading this I am still there for those around me and still show up every day as a partner, mother, daughter, sister and friend if needed by those I love, this is not about abandoning people.

Looking back on my life, I am surprised that it took me until my fifties to fully embrace self-love. It is something I wish I had discovered earlier, but I do not regret my journey. I know that self-love is not about perfection, it is a lifelong commitment to myself.

If you are reading this and you are still on the path toward self-love, know this: you are enough. You do not have to be perfect. You do not have to have everything figured out. The process of learning to love yourself is worth every step, every challenge, and every setback. It is the key to living a fulfilled and happy life.

I may be a slow learner, but I am learning. I am a work in progress and as I continue along, I remind myself that I am worthy of love, happiness, and peace.

11

Becoming Someone New

Change wasn't a choice for me it was a necessity if I wanted to live a long healthy life. This chapter embraces what it took to transform, live with resilience, and the freedom of rewriting my own story.

Through this difficult journey, I learnt an important lesson: If I didn't learn to love and care for myself, I couldn't truly show up for the people I loved. The relationship I had with myself was foundational to everything else. The love I was seeking from others had to come from within me first. I couldn't expect anyone else to give me the love, care, and validation I wasn't giving myself.

It has been a long journey, and I still face challenges. But looking back, I realise that everything I went through and the struggles were all part of the process of reclaiming myself. I had to go through the pain, the confusion, and the self-doubt to come out the other side stronger, wiser, and more in tune with who I truly am.

The importance good health is something I now understand deeply, but it took a crisis to open my eyes. Understanding that my mental health wasn't just about recognising when something was wrong. It was about understanding the critical role this played in every aspect of my life, from my mind, physical health to my relationships and my overall quality of life.

What do I mean by this?

Mental health refers to a person's emotional, psychological, and social wellbeing. It influences how we think, feel, and behave, and affects how we handle life's everyday challenges, form relationships, and make decisions. Good mental health helps people to work productively, realise their potential, and cope with stress in a healthy and sustainable way. According to Beyond Blue and the Australian Department of Health, mental health is about overall wellbeing and the capacity to enjoy life.

Mental and physical health are deeply connected, and both are essential to a person's overall wellbeing. When we take care of both our mind and body, we're better equipped to manage stress, connect with others, and contribute to our families, workplaces, and communities. On the other hand, when health is neglected, we can begin to feel physically drained and emotionally overwhelmed. The pressures of work, family commitments, and social expectations can feel relentless, making it hard to find enjoyment or a sense of balance in daily life.

If our mental or physical health is suffering, it can have a ripple effect. Feelings of exhaustion, lack of motivation, or disconnection may start to take over. However, when we actively prioritise our mental and physical wellbeing, it becomes easier to stay grounded, present, and connected both with ourselves and those around us. Focusing on wellbeing is not selfish; it's essential. It allows us to build resilience, improve our relationships, and engage more fully in the things that matter most.

— **Beyond Blue** and the
Australian Department of Health

Your Body: Chronic stress, anxiety, and depression can take a serious toll on your body. It can lead to burnout, weakened immune systems, digestive issues, weight gain, and even more severe conditions like heart disease. Your body and mind are connected, and when one suffers, the other follows.

Your Mind: When you're stressed or overwhelmed, it's harder to be present with the people you love. Your relationships can suffer when you're constantly running on empty. Taking care of your mental health helps you be more patient, more understanding, and more connected to others.

Your Soul: When you take care of your mind, you're able to focus better and work more efficiently. You make better decisions, and your creativity thrives. Mental well-being isn't just about avoiding burnout; it's about improving your capacity for success. When you have joy in your soul you have joy in your life.

I have experienced firsthand the consequences of neglecting my health. I pushed myself for years, thinking that if I just kept going, everything would work out. But the truth is, it wasn't sustainable. It took a life-threatening illness for me to realise the price I almost paid.

So, what happens if you don't make mental and physical health a priority?

You risk burnout, physical illness, strained relationships, and a complete loss of joy and purpose. You become disconnected from yourself, and everything becomes a chore. You may find yourself stuck in a cycle of exhaustion, guilt, and frustration. You may even reach a point where your body forces you to slow down, as it did for me.

But it doesn't have to get to that point.

By making the conscious decision to choose yourself today, you can create a healthier, happier life. You can avoid stress, illness and burnout, build stronger relationships, and find joy in the everyday moments. It's never too late to make a change.

Just as the analogy of "fitting your oxygen mask first before assisting others" comes from airline safety instructions, where passengers are advised to secure their own oxygen mask before helping others in case of an emergency. It emphasises the idea that you need to take care of yourself first before you can effectively help others.

In a broader sense, this concept is often used to stress the importance of self-care and mental well-being. If you're not in a stable condition—whether physically, emotionally, or mentally you won't be able to provide support or care for others in a meaningful way. It's like ensuring your own "health" or "resources" are in place so you can be of service to others without draining yourself.

The first step is acknowledging you need to do this. Its hard embarrassing and means you need to be accountable to yourself. For a long time, I was listening to my internal dialogue and creating a world in my head that did not require me to change anything. The little voice the one we've all got, the one that says "yes you have had a hard day today you deserve that drink tonight and makes it alright to reward yourself after a hard day with some bad food to accompany it. You don't need to go for a walk or exercise just put in another hour of work, as I must keep looking like I am a superstar I really care about what others think of me."

Here is a starting point remember small changes will eventually create large changes and good habits.

Self-Care Starter – Because It's Time to Begin!
Take a moment today to reflect: What can you do for yourself right now to nurture your mental health?

1. **Self-Awareness:**
   Start by tuning in to your feelings, energy, and stress levels. Recognise when you're feeling overwhelmed or drained and give yourself permission to rest. Knowing what you need is the first step toward caring for yourself.

What is one thing you can do today to become more aware of your emotions or energy levels?

_____

2. **Healthy Boundaries:**
   Learn the power of saying no when you're stretched too thin. Protect your mental health by recognising your limits and asking for help when needed. It's okay not to do everything.

What is one boundary you can set today to protect your well-being?

3. **Mindfulness and Meditation:**
   These simple practices can help quiet your mind, reduce stress, and improve focus. Even taking a few minutes a day to centre yourself can foster a sense of calm and clarity.

How can you incorporate a few minutes of mindfulness or meditation into your day?

___

4. **Making Time for You:**
   Amid life's demands, don't forget to prioritise activities that bring you joy. Self-care isn't selfish; it's necessary. Regularly engaging in what you love will help you recharge.

What is one activity you can do today that brings you joy?

___

5. **Ask for Support:**
   If you're struggling, seek support. Whether it's a therapist, a trusted friend, or a coach, asking for help shows strength, not weakness. You don't have to navigate everything alone.

Who is one person you can reach out to for support?

Not everyone can recover from a bad health diagnosis.

Prevention is essential to living a balanced, fulfilling life. Today, I know that taking care of my mind, body and soul is a priority and a path to a well fulfilling future life.

All of us in some way or at some time have thought it will never happen to me!

Well I don't want it to happen to anyone and that has been the motivation to share my story in this book and if it somehow makes one person stop and make changes to their mind, body and soul health then it has been worth the hours it has taken me to put all of my lived experiences onto these pages.

If you're reading this and you're caught in a cycle of overwork, exhaustion, and guilt, know that you don't have to keep living this way. There is a better way you can create a life that's not only successful but also meaningful, joyful, and fulfilling. Often we wait for trauma loss, illness or tragedy before initiating any change.

12

Feedback, What Others See and What I Know

In today's world, feedback is almost inescapable — it's embedded in everything from our workplace performance to the online services we use daily. Whether it's a customer leaving a one-star rating on Google reviews or a manager discussing KPIs during an employment evaluation, the intention behind feedback is often to inform improvement. Social media, too, has become a place where feedback is instant and public, think of the comments under a business's Instagram post or a viral TikTok video. Navigating this feedback, particularly when it feels negative or personal, can be challenging.

From my own perspective, I've come to see feedback not as a personal attack, but as an opportunity for a conversation or reflection and growth. In the past I have struggled and found it easy to feel criticised, especially when comments weren't delivered tactfully. Over time, I am still learning to filter out what's constructive from what's simply noise.

An example of this is: A blunt employment review might highlight areas for development, but rather than taking it as a character judgement, I will now question, "What is this really telling me about how I work and how I can improve?"

In my experience this is much harder to receive and navigate when it is the written word and not given in person. The reason is that you cannot see the expression or emotion it has been delivered with.

It's also important to consider the intent behind the feedback. A customer review on Google may be sharp or poorly worded, but at its core could be a genuine issue that needs attention. In contrast, online comments can sometimes cross the line into trolling or unhelpful criticism. Learning to distinguish between the two is essential. I try to approach all feedback with curiosity first, even if my instinct is to feel defensive.

By asking questions, requesting examples, or even just taking a moment to breathe before reacting, I am learning to use feedback to my advantage without feeling targeted and attacked. This has altered how I allow it to affect me and how I respond.

Modern KPIs and performance tools have made feedback more data-driven, which can be useful, but they also risk feeling impersonal. That's why it's crucial to combine metrics with meaningful conversation. I believe that, when delivered respectfully, feedback whether from an algorithm, a manager, or an online reviewer can be very powerful.

Even more powerful when it is received with an open mind, it's not a threat, but a mirror that helps us sharpen our strengths and address our blind spots.

Negative feedback is an opportunity to grow!

Positive feedback is an opportunity to take pride in ourselves!

Alongside external feedback, I've also come to value the role of self-evaluation perhaps even more so. Over the past few years, I've had to learn how to be honest with myself without being harsh. Living with an ostomy bag has changed not only how I see myself physically, but how I relate to the world around me. It's easy to focus on what makes you different, especially when you're adapting to something as personal and visible as a change in appearance. But self-evaluation has taught me that difference isn't deficiency it's part of my story, and it deserves space without shame or pity from others.

There were times when my internal voice became my biggest critic. It wasn't just about appearance; it was the discomfort, the adjustments, and the constant negotiation with what used to feel effortless. But I've learned that self-evaluation doesn't have to mean picking yourself apart. It can mean recognising how resilient you've become, how much you've adapted, and how you continue to show up despite things being harder than they were before. That's a kind of strength that no external review could ever fully capture.

It sometimes requires kindness, focusing on how far you've come. Looking at the big picture not the small negative things that need improvement as they will always be a work in progress, this kind of evaluation is key to moving forward. Give yourself positive feed back and feel proud of your progress no matter how small. Change the internal dialogue.

I now try to approach self-feedback with the same care and balance that I hope for from others. Yes, I reflect on what I could do differently whether that's how I manage my energy, my mindset, or my physical needs and yes, I can always improve. I also make space to acknowledge what I'm doing well. Just as with professional KPIs or social media comments, it's about identifying what's useful and leaving behind what's just noise.

Ultimately, feedback whether from others or from within is part of a broader journey of self-awareness. Living with an ostomy has taught me that growth isn't always about fixing something; sometimes it's about learning to live well with what is. And for me, that's what feedback is about not perfection, but progress, understanding, and compassion, both from others and within myself.

Every challenge presents a new perspective, and every piece of feedback — whether from a colleague, a stranger online, or my own inner voice — can be a doorway to something else. It doesn't mean I have to agree with everything I hear, but it does mean I can choose to make improvements a choice with how I respond, identifying how I carry that learning forward. There's real power in this, the power to keep evolving, even in the face of things we never expected to face.

Using feedback towards professional growth, motivating us to push and question boundaries with no limit to what we can achieve, knowing that our efforts are recognised and appreciated.

In our personal life, feedback plays a similarly important role. Think about the last time someone praised you for something you did for them whether it was a kind gesture, a thoughtful word, or a show of support. When you receive positive feedback, it doesn't just feel good in the moment; it creates a sense of satisfaction and drives us to continue this behaviour. If our friends or family regularly express appreciation for the effort we put into a relationship, we are more likely to continue investing in it, finding ways to improve communication, deepen connections, and demonstrate care.

> *It is crucial that such compliments are sincere and reflect your true feelings. Authenticity ensures the feedback is meaningful and well-received. Effective feedback should be genuine, specific, and respectful, enhancing the well-being of both the giver and the receiver.*
>
> *By offering heartfelt feedback, we not only brighten someone's day but also contribute to a culture of kindness and positivity in our communities.*
> **— *Time* magazine**

In personal relationships, romantic, or platonic feedback is vital for maintaining healthy and strong connections. It helps to address misunderstandings, prevent resentment, and foster open communication. Without feedback, relationships can become stagnant, and unspoken issues can fester, leading to unnecessary conflict.

In personal life, constructive feedback should be given with care and consideration.

To fully benefit from feedback, I have learnt that it is crucial to shift my mindset from viewing it as criticism to seeing it as a tool for growth. It's easy to become defensive or dismissive when receiving feedback that is uncomfortable, but doing so can limit personal development.

Instead, make sure you approach feedback with curiosity and a desire to learn more about yourself.

One way to embrace feedback is to practise self-reflection. After receiving feedback, take time to reflect on it before reacting. Ask yourself questions like, "Why did this feedback resonate with me?" or "What changes can I make based on this input?" This reflective approach allows you to process feedback calmly and thoughtfully, leading to more positive outcomes.

By embracing feedback with openness and a growth mindset, we can transform it from a mere tool into an ongoing practice that enriches our lives. Whether from a friend, family member, or partner, feedback is a gift that, when received thoughtfully, can help us reach our full potential.

As an experiment for this book, I have put myself in line for some genuine feedback:

I have been vulnerable by asking some of those close to me, family and friends to provide feedback honestly and openly.

I have asked them all the same highlighted question below and have not changed their responses just printed them as they were given to me anonymously and in no specific order:

"Considering where I am now, how do you see my transformation towards a healthier and less stressful life?"

Person 1 - Positive:
You have chosen to change your diet, your environment as well as who you surround yourself with. You choose things like yoga and meditation to calm your mind so you can be the best version of yourself.

Person 1 - Negative:
Not being as close with your children due to living further away.

Person 2 - Positive:
Living near the beach, healthy environment, improved health both physical and mental!

Person 2 - Negative:
Giving up relationships, friendships and previous lifestyle.

Person 3 - Positive:
What I have seen you accomplish in a short time once you decided to commit to the change has been transformative and inspiring. You're clear on what you want every day to look like, so you live your best life.

Person 3 - Negative:
You should have done it sooner, you are more relaxed, worrying less about the little things and worrying less about the things that are beyond your control. You've always been beautiful inside and out but now there is an extra glow.

Person 4 - Positive:
The mental and emotional state that you have achieved has been far better than if you had never tried to make changes.

Personal 4 - Negative:
You fixate on the fact you have finally found happiness and peace, but the people you meet the challenges you have overcome are often more valuable and meaningful than the destination itself. "It's the not about the destination it's the journey that matters more so focus on the journey."

Person 5 - Positive:
Strength, resilience, and focus on your personal goals and creating the life you want, such as making space to travel and stepping out of your comfort zone to meet new people and moving.

Person 5 - Negative:
Sometimes focusing only on the positive can be just as damaging. All emotions are valid. There can be greater power in accepting and acknowledging where we are at and how we respond.

Person 6 - Positive:
You have rebuilt not only your internal soul, but you have also made sure the shell we all refer to as the body has been transformed, you have chosen to be present in the moment with your mind and all of this has taken shape. You have won the trifecta. You do not look your age, your persona is young and vibrant, and you bring fun, love and laughter along with positive and engaging energy to everyone you meet and most of all you are not afraid to tell your story.

Person 6 - Negative:
While your transformation has been your personal goal, there may become from time to time a risk of overextending yourself and falling back into bad habits of wanting to be everything to everyone and forgetting the work you have done on yourself.

Even in this calmer chapter of your life, it's clear that your past experiences, where you wore many hats, which shaped you into the resilient person you are today does not creep back. Do not allow one hick up to undo all the work and where you may feel the pressure of people pleasing and "doing it all" takes over.

It's important that, as you continue your healing journey, you also take time to just exist, without any expectations or duties attached.

As you have seen from the feedback provided there is no right or wrong it can also be objective due to individual values, for example one persons negative can be someone else's positive it is all just feedback, right? Looking at the subjects raised there are some definite areas for improvement that I can work on. Equally I can feel great about some of the feedback provided to encourage me to keep going. Feedback can be given and received the information is your own and it is entirely up to each of us individuals what we choose to do with the information. It is however an important skill to be able to graciously accept feedback as it can be an effective tool used for personal growth.

13

Everything I Was, Everything I Now Am

This is the final chapter bringing it all together grief and gratitude, pain and progress. A reflection on my identity and the beautiful complexity of my survival as the butterfly has now emerged. I am safe in the knowledge that you have never really arrived life is a journey not a destination I still have much work to accomplish, both helping others and myself. We are all a work in progress.

I WAS

I was stressed. Every day felt like a pressure cooker, the lid about to blow off with the weight of my responsibilities, my ambitions, my fears. The constant deadlines, the never-ending to-do lists, the relentless pursuit of more, more, more. No matter how much I achieved, it never felt like enough. I was a negative person, clouded by doubts that followed me like shadows, always lurking, always whispering that I wasn't good enough. I was driven by money and success, believing that these would fill the void within me, give me purpose, and perhaps finally make me worthy of respect and admiration, believing that reaching a destination or goal would then make life better.

But I couldn't see it then. I couldn't see the toll it was taking on my future self the sacrifices, the compromises, the pieces of my soul that I was offering up to a never-ending cycle of ambition. I was always seeking, craving approval from people I barely knew, from society, from the world at large. I lived a life not for myself, but to please others, to meet their expectations, to be what they wanted me to be.

I was living a life for external validation, not for internal fulfillment. I had no idea of my own worth beyond what others told me I was worth. It took a cancer diagnosis not once, but twice to wake me up. Those moments, sitting in sterile hospital rooms, hair falling out, mind racing, gave me a terrifying, yet awakening clarity. I was reminded that life is fragile. But despite that reminder, I kept pushing. I kept running the same race, repeating the same patterns, thinking that if I just worked harder, tried to do more, everything would fall into place.

But in truth, I wasn't living I was merely existing. I wasn't showing up for myself; I was just going through the motions. I was repeating old patterns, patterns of self-doubt, fear, exhaustion, and self-sabotage. I was damaging my mind, body, and soul in ways I couldn't even understand yet. And deep down, I knew it wasn't right. I was someone I didn't like, someone who forgot how to be kind to themselves. I was starting to question it all, wondering if this was the life I was supposed to lead, if this was the person I was meant to be.

I LEARNT

It wasn't until I hit rock bottom that I truly began to see. Slowly, painfully, I started to learn. I learnt that my family are always there for me, no matter what. In my darkest moments, when I felt utterly alone, they were the ones who held me up. They stood beside me when I had nothing left to give, offering me love, comfort, and strength, even when I felt weak. I learnt that friends can be the most generous, giving souls, people who would drop everything to support me, to listen, to offer their hearts in a way that made me realise the true meaning of friendship.

I learnt to trust the universe and its path, even when it didn't make sense. I didn't understand why these challenges were happening to me, but I started to trust that they were there to teach me something important, to lead me somewhere better, even if I couldn't see it at the time. I learnt to slow down and be grateful for what I had, rather than constantly chasing the next big thing. I realised that I didn't need more success or more money to feel rich. I needed good health, family, and friends. That, for me now, is true wealth.

I learnt that when life knocks you down, you get back up again. And I don't just mean physically, I mean emotionally, mentally, spiritually. Cancer tried to break me, but I got back up, time and time again, even when it seemed impossible.

I learnt that bald women can still be beautiful, no matter what. At first, I looked in the mirror and saw only loss—my hair, my energy, my old self. But in time, I saw strength, resilience, and a raw kind of beauty that came from within.

I learnt that living a slower life is not lazy; it's necessary. Slowing down didn't mean I wasn't ambitious or driven. It meant I was learning how to truly live in the present, to embrace the moments that truly mattered.

I learnt that self-love is not selfish it is essential. It's the foundation of everything else. You cannot give from an empty cup.

I learnt that what you think, you create. I saw the truth in this as I started to change the way I thought about myself, about my life. When I changed my mindset, I began to see the world differently. I learnt that you attract what you feel.

I learnt that what you imagine, you become. The power of our imagination is staggering. I could visualise the kind of person I wanted to be, the life I wanted to lead, and I realised I had the ability to make it happen.

I learnt that what you desire in life is possible. It may not come immediately, and it may take longer than expected, but if you're patient and persistent, what you want can become your reality.

I learnt to be accountable to myself. No one could fix me but me. It was up to me to change my circumstances, to stop blaming the world, or others, or fate.

I learnt to rest without guilt, to take moments to recharge, to stop feeling like I always had to be "doing." I learnt to have a quiet mind, to shut out the noise of the world, and just be.

I learnt to have meaningful conversations, ones that connect, that matter. I stopped wasting time on small talk and started investing in conversations that would nurture my soul.

I have learnt that calm and quiet is not boring it's healing. The world is loud, and it pulls us in so many directions. But in the quiet, in the stillness, I found my peace.

I learnt that the greatest wealth you will ever have in life is a healthy body. Without it, all the money in the world means nothing.

I learnt that intimacy can be the meeting of two minds no need for grand gestures, just true connection, an understanding that transcends words.

I have learnt that stepping outside your comfort zone is where the good stuff is. The magic happens when you challenge yourself, when you push past your fears, when you do the things that scare you. I have learnt that everything happens so that we can grow. The challenges, the struggles, the pain they were all opportunities in disguise.

I have learnt that a lot goes wrong before it goes right. Growth is messy, and sometimes it feels like everything is falling apart, but I now understand that it's all part of the process.

I learnt not to force things to work out. Some things will fall into place naturally, and others won't. I can't control everything, and I don't need to.

I learnt to accept happiness and joy back into my life. For so long, I had pushed joy away, not feeling worthy of it. But I now know that happiness is my birthright.

I learnt that there are no mistakes, only lessons. Every misstep, every failure, has been a lesson, a stepping stone that has brought me closer to who I am meant to be.

I learnt not to speak negatively about myself. Words have power. The things I say to myself shape my reality. I learnt to understand myself, to stop judging myself so harshly, and to recognise my worth.

I learnt that being alone is a powerful tool in understanding yourself. Solitude is not loneliness; it's an opportunity to discover who you truly are when the noise of the world falls away.

I learnt that I cannot control other people's actions or words. I cannot control how others see me or what they think of me. But I can control my own actions, my own words, and my own responses. I have learnt to love myself not just in the easy moments, but especially in the hard ones. Self-love isn't about perfection; it's about acceptance.

I learnt that diet and exercise really are key ingredients to a long healthy lifestyle. Not just words in a lifestyle magazine, Instagram post or on a TV show.

I have learnt that I will never stop learning. Life is a journey, and every day brings new opportunities for growth, self-discovery, and transformation.

I AM

And now, I stand here stronger than I ever imagined I could be. I never knew I had this much strength within me. Every challenge, every trial, has shaped me into someone resilient, someone who knows how to rise. I am happier than I ever thought possible. Happiness doesn't come from external circumstances, but from within. I have learnt how to cultivate it, how to find joy in the simplest of things.

I am healing every single day. The process isn't linear, and some days are harder than others, but every day, I am moving closer to the person I am meant to be. I am healthy, mind, body, and soul. My body is no longer something I abuse in the name of ambition. It's my temple, and I treat it with the love and respect it deserves.

I am cancer-free. I am not defined by what I've been through, but by how I've overcome it. I am turning my life on its head in a positive way. The person I was no longer controls me. I am taking control of my story, rewriting it with purpose, with intention. I am in control of my own reactions and words. I no longer allow the world to dictate how I feel or how I respond. I am seeing the world with new eyes, eyes that are grateful, eyes that are present.

I am proud of me. Not because I've achieved everything, I set out to do, but because I have come this far. I am exactly where I am supposed to be right now. Every step, every stumble, every lesson has brought me here and for that, I am grateful.

I am no longer the person I once was. I am stronger, wiser, more at peace with myself than I ever thought possible. This is my story. And I'm just getting started.

I am living life for the greater good of me.

You also deserve to be well, and you deserve to live a healthy life!

Take the time to care for yourself. Your future self will thank you for it.

Much Love Nic x

Afterword

Thank you for reading until the end of my book, what most people don't realise is this is not really the end of the story for anyone like me, anyone who has gone through serious illness is changed forever.

We will never be who we were before. There is a constant fear always in our thoughts, the mental toll is huge and our bodies have been through so much. We live on a rollercoaster we never asked to ride, and we can't get off! Any small sign of being unwell, or a change in any part of our body triggers a silent trauma and fear response that we all feel and most never speak of. Life is now measured with scans, tests, the time between appointments, Just waiting for these results each time is all consuming, emotional and exhausting.

I am well, and I am living my best life. But that life now exists in six-month blocks. I am only ever as good as my next scan, my next blood test, my next appointment. Each time I walk into that room, my oncologist holds my future in his hands not metaphorically, but literally. And until he speaks, I don't know whether I've been handed another six months of life, or something altogether different.

That moment the time between having the tests and hearing the results is almost unbearable. A week of holding your breath. A week of carrying the weight of your own mortality, over and over again. You hope. You believe. You pray. But deep down, tucked away in the furthest corner of your mind, you know you must be ready if the news isn't good. The emotional strength it takes to prepare yourself for either outcome, time and time again, is beyond description.

I often feel sick as I step out of the car. My eyes well up. I fight back the tears, put on a brave face, smile at the receptionist, make polite conversation, and take my seat in that waiting room alongside others on the same journey. Young, old, visibly unwell or not, we all sit in quiet solidarity, sometimes sharing a knowing smile, sometimes just holding our own space, waiting to hear how our next chapter will be written.

And then I'm called in.

He sits, focused, staring at the screen reading the results that will determine the next part of my life. That moment, for me, is everything. It's either a golden ticket or a sentence. But no matter what, I'm always grateful for him, for the science, for the people who have made it possible for me to still be here. He has saved my life, twice. And I don't take that for granted. I often think about what it must be like for him delivering good news, yes, but also devastating news. What a heavy, bittersweet privilege he carries. I thank him silently every time for his years of study, his commitment to his field, and the part he plays in the research that keeps people like me alive.

But none of this ever gets easier. It doesn't soften with time. Because I know all too well it was fifteen years between the first diagnosis and the second. Nothing is certain. Nothing is promised.

We all know someone who's been through this. But it's important to understand we are never truly "fixed". We are never the same. This is our new normal. And if you're reading this, and you've been there, or you are there now please know that I see you and feel what you are experiencing. You are not alone we are so many people.

This is my truth. My new normal, this is my life. Six months at a time but most importantly I'm still here.

About the Author

Nicole Trimboli is a speaker, wellness mentor, and meditation teacher whose work is grounded in lived experience. As a Lived Experience Committee Member at the Bowel Cancer Outcomes Registry (BCOR) and a Coloplast Ambassador, Nicole brings deep personal insight into the challenges and opportunities of health recovery and wellbeing. She is passionate about helping others prioritise their wellbeing, embrace preventative and holistic practices, and reconnect with a life of meaning, balance, and self-care.

Nicole's journey into wellness wasn't born out of curiosity it was born out of necessity. After being diagnosed with cancer in 2006 and again in 2021, she was forced to stop, reassess her life, and make profound changes in how she lived, thought, and cared for herself. What followed was not only physical healing, but a complete transformation of her mindset and lifestyle.

For years, Nicole lived what many would call a successful life thriving in high-pressure corporate environments, raising her family, and giving tirelessly to everyone around her. But like so many, she placed herself last, her own health, mental and physical wellbeing quietly pushed aside. It took a two life-threatening diagnosis for her to realise the toll this had taken.

Today, Nicole is well and living her best life, but that life now exists in six-month blocks. She is only ever as good as her next scan, her next blood test, her next appointment. Each time she walks into that room, her oncologist holds her future in his hands not metaphorically, but literally. Until he speaks, she doesn't know whether she's been granted another six months of life or something altogether different.

Grateful for the science, her surgeon and oncologist who have as a team saved her life twice.

Nicole knows this too well that nothing is guaranteed, it was fifteen years between her first diagnosis and her second. Tomorrow is promised to no one, and she is not alone. There are so many walking this same path.

Through her work and this book, Nicole hopes to show others that true healing goes far beyond the body. It's about mindset, emotional resilience, and a deep commitment to caring for oneself. She doesn't call herself a coach she's someone who walks beside others with empathy, sharing tools, stories and strategies from her own lived experience.

She knows what it's like to live a "crazy busy" life, to always be rushing, to put everyone else first. And now, with honesty and warmth, she helps others step off that treadmill and begin again with clarity, balance, and kindness towards themselves.

Writing this book has been an emotional journey revisiting the hardest parts of her life, while also celebrating the strength it took to survive them. It's a reminder that healing is never one thing, never one moment but it is always possible.

Nicole's purpose, shaped by her own lived experience, is to support and uplift others both those navigating illness themselves and those walking beside a loved one through it. Her mission is to ensure that no one feels invisible, unheard, or alone on their journey.

"Because shit shows don't have to be the end of your story"

Nicole Trimboli

Speaker Bio

Nicole Trimboli is an author, speaker, and wellness mentor with a deep commitment to empowering others through the lens of lived experience. Drawing on her current roles as a Lived Experience Committee Member for the Bowel Cancer Outcomes Registry (BCOR) and Coloplast Ambassador, Nicole shares powerful personal insights into navigating health challenges and cultivating resilience. Her work encourages audiences to embrace preventative self-care, prioritise wellbeing, and foster a more mindful, balanced life.

Nicole is now the author of **What A Sh!t Show**—a powerful and relatable account of what it means to face life when everything seems to fall apart. Drawing from her own story, she speaks openly about the messiness of life, the moments we don't post on social media, and the "shit shows" that shape us. Because the truth is we've all had one. Or several.

Her own journey into wellness wasn't a gentle nudge it was a full stop. After being diagnosed with cancer in 2006 and again in 2021, Nicole was forced to reassess everything. What followed was more than just physical recovery it was a total transformation of how she lived, thought, and cared for herself.

Now living with a stoma and an ostomy bag, Nicole shares her experience with openness to reduce stigma and foster connection. She also serves as a lived experience committee member for the **Bowel Cancer Outcomes Registry**, using her experience to help improve outcomes for so many others. In addition Nicole provides peer support and insiration to others living with an ostomy through her role as an Ambassador for **Coloplast Pty Ltd**.

Before her diagnosis, Nicole thrived in high-pressure corporate environments while raising a family and giving endlessly to everyone but herself. Like so many, she put herself last. It took two life-threatening wake-up calls to understand the cost of living that way.

Today, she lives well but in six-month blocks, measured between scans and blood tests. It's a life lived with gratitude and presence, shaped by the knowledge that nothing is guaranteed.

Nicole doesn't call herself a coach. She leads by example and walks beside people with honesty, warmth, and empathy offering practical tools, lived wisdom, and the space to breathe again. Her mission is to ensure no one feels invisible, unheard, or alone whether they are facing illness themselves or supporting someone who is.

Because yes, life can be a shit show. But healing, hope, and humour still live there too!

www.nicoletrimboli.com.au

Instagram - @nicoletrimboliwellness

Instagram - @nicolewhatash1tshow

YouTube - @nicolewhatash1tshow

References

Australian Institute of Health and Welfare – Australian govt.
Australian Quality Clinical Audit reports
Marcus Aurelius, Meditations, Book 6, Section 30
Harvard Health
Benchpress
Psychology Today
Coloplast Pty Ltd
Hollister
PMC (PubMed Central)
Beyond Blue
Australian Department of Health

References

Acknowledgements

I would like to express my deepest gratitude to the many individuals and teams who supported me throughout my shit show—both in life and in bringing this book to completion.

Mr Ravish Jootun & Mitcham Healthcare
Laparoscopic, Endoscopic, and Robotic Surgeon
Ravish thank you for your life-saving surgeries. Your skill and dedication gave me a second chance. With special mention to the caring and kind **Monique**—your compassion made all the difference during difficult times.

Dr Prasad Cooray & Yarra Oncology Team
Medical Oncologist
Prasad thank you for your expertise life-saving chemotherapy treatment and ongoing support. With heartfelt thanks to **Mel**, my chemotherapy nurse at Knox Private—your kindness and care were a constant source of strength.

Knox Private Hospital – Waratah Ward
To **Tess** and **Greg**, and your incredibly dedicated team of nurses: you helped me through some of the most difficult days I have ever faced. "Thank you" will never be enough, and you will never be forgotten.

A special mention to **Alison and Kate**, my stoma nurses—your ongoing support in helping me adjust to life with a stoma and ileostomy bag has meant the world.

Dr Winnie Cheng & Dr Lin Chaung
Heathmont General Practice
Thank you both for being my loyal doctors for over 25 years I have such appreciation for you always going above and beyond with your care for me through it all!

Creative and Publishing Team

Editor
Victoria – for your guidance and insight in shaping this manuscript.

Cover Design
Nikola Boskovski – for beautifully capturing the essence of this book.

Layout and Typesetting
Ultimate World Publishing – for your professionalism and care in presenting this work.

Photography
Sarah Cogger / Sarah Frank Photography
www.sarahfrankphotographer.com
Thank you for a front cover that says it all! Your images carry both meaning and emotion.

Publisher
Ultimate World Publishing – your structure and the amazing team of people helped bring this book to life.

Notes

www.ingramcontent.com/pod-product-compliance
Lightning Source LLC
Chambersburg PA
CBHW060451080526
44584CB00015B/1403